Reading for TODAY

Book One

Program Authors

**Linda Ward Beech • James Beers • Jo Ann Dauzat
Sam V. Dauzat • Tara McCarthy**

Program Consultants

Myra K. Baum
Office of Adult and
   Continuing Education
Brooklyn, New York

Francis J. Feltman, Jr.
Racine Youth Offender
   Correctional Facility
Racine, Wisconsin

Mary Ann Guilliams
Gary Job Corps
San Marcos, Texas

Julie Jacobs
Inmate Literacy Project
Santa Clara County Library
Milpitas, California

Maxine L. McCormick
Workforce Education
Orange County Public Schools
Orlando, Florida

Sandra S. Owens
Laurens County Literacy Council
Laurens, South Carolina

STECK-VAUGHN
ELEMENTARY · SECONDARY · ADULT · LIBRARY

A Harcourt Company

www.steck-vaughn.com

Acknowledgments

Staff Credits

Executive Editor: Ellen Northcutt
Senior Editor: Donna Townsend
Associate Design Director: Joyce Spicer
Supervising Designer: Pamela Heaney
Designer: Jessica Bristow
Production Coordinator: Rebecca Gonzales
Electronic Production Artists: Julia Miracle-Hagaman and Karen Wilburn
Senior Technical Advisor: Alan Klemp
Electronic Production Specialist: Dina Bahan

Photography Credits

Photography by Park Street Photography; Digital Studios, Austin, Texas; Artville; Corbis; Eyewire; iSwoop; PhotoDisc; and Eyewire.

Cover: (bus) Ken Lax, (men working), Dan Cohen, (fixing tire) Tomás Ovalle; (carrying boxes) Ken Walker; p.1 (bee) ©Stephen Dalton/Animals Animals; p.2 (hug) ©Jose Pelaez Photography/The Stock Market; p.2 (gate) ©Robert W. Ginn/Unicorn Stock Photos; p.3 (money) ©John Neubauer/PhotoEdit; p.4 (sick) ©Alan Thomton/Stone; p.7 (vane) ©Charles D. Winters/Photo Researchers, Inc.; p.7 (game) ©John Lei/Stock Boston; p.7 (gate) ©Robert W. Ginn/Unicorn Stock Photos; p.8 (vane) ©Charles D. Winters/Photo Researchers, Inc.; p.9 (fin) ©Gerard Lacz/Peter Arnold, Inc.; p.9 (sick) ©Alan Thomton/Stone; p.9 (igloo) ©David Roseberg/Stone; p.10 (hive) ©Ken Stepnell/Bruce Coleman, Inc.; p.11 (fin) ©Gerard Lacz/Peter Arnold, Inc.; p.13 (ox) ©Russell Grunake/Unicorn Stock Photos; p.16 (hug) ©Jose Pelaez Photography/The Stock Market; p.16 (judge) ©Dennis MacDonald/Unicorn Stock Photos; p.17 (flute) ©Park Street; p.18 (hug) ©Jose Pelaez Photography/The Stock Market; p.21 (seal) ©Fred Bruemmer/Peter Arnold, Inc.; p.21 (weed) ©Gabe Palmer/The Stock Market; p.21 (seed) ©Maximilian Stock LTD/Earth Scenes; p.21 (team) ©Robert E. Daemmrich/Stone; p.21 (bee) ©Stephen Dalton/Animals Animals; p.22 (seal) ©Fred Bruemmer/Peter Arnold, Inc.; p.22 (weed) ©Gabe Palmer/The Stock Market; p.24 Jeff Gritchen; p.25 (b) Ken Walker; p.25 (c) ©David Young-Wolff/PhotoEdit; p.25 (d) Jeff Gritchen; p.26 Christine Galida; p.28 Jeff Gritchen; p.29 (a) Christine Galida; p.29 (b) ©Myrleen Ferguson/PhotoEdit; p.29 (c) Jeff Gritchen; p.29 (d) Park Street; p.29 (e) ©David Young-Wolff/PhotoEdit; p.29 (g) ©Tony Freeman/PhotoEdit; p.30 (a) Park Street; p.30 (b) Christine Galida; p.30 (d) Jeff Gritchen; p.30 (f) Dan Cohen; p.30 (g) ©Stone; p.31 (a) ©Charles Gupton/Stock Boston; p.31 (b) ©Tony Freeman/PhotoEdit; p.31 (c) Dan Cohen; p.31 (d) Ken Lax; p.32 Rick Williams; p.34 Rick Williams; p.35 (b) ©John Neubauer/PhotoEdit; p.35 (c) Christine Galida; p.35 (e) Ken Walker; p.36 Rick Williams; p.37 (a, e) Ken Lax; p.37 (c) Rick Williams; p.38 (b) ©Daemmrich/Stock Boston; p.38 (c) Christine Galida; p.38 (d) Park Street; p.38 (e) Ken Walker; p.38 (f) ©Tim Davis/Stone; p.39 (a) Tomás Ovalle; p.39 (b) ©Fotographica/CORBIS; p.39 (c, e) Christina Galida; p.39 (d) Ken Walker; p.40 Tomás Ovalle; p.42 Ken Walker; p.44 Tomás Ovalle; p.45 (a) ©Daemmrich/Stock Boston; p.45 (b, e) Ken Lax; p.45 (c) Christine Galida; p.45 (d) Rick Williams; p.45 (g) Dan Cohen; p.45 (h) Jeff Gritchen; p.46 (a) ©Superstock; p.46 (e, f, g) Jeff Gritchen; p.47 (a) ©Lawrence Migdale/Stock Boston; p.47 (b, c, d) Jeff Gritchen; p.47 (e) Christine Galida; p.47 (f) ©Bob Daemmrich/Stock Boston; pp.47 (g), 48, 49 (a, b, c, d, e) Park Street; p.50 Christine Galida; p.51 (a, c, d) Ken Lax; p.52 (a, b) Rick Williams; p.54 (a) ©Peter Southwick/Stock Boston; p.55 (a, c, f, i) Christina Galida; p.55 (b) Park Street; p.55 (e, h) Dan Cohen; pp.55 (g), 56 (a) Rick Williams; p.56 (b, c, e) Park Street; p.56 (f) Tomás Ovalle; p.56 (g) Christine Galida; p.57 Ken Lax; p.60 (b) ©Superstock; p.61 (a) Tomás Ovalle; p.61 (b) Dan Cohen; p.61 (c) Park Street; p.61 (d) Christine Galida; p.62 (a) Dan Cohen; p.62 (c) Christine Galida; p.62 (d, e) Ken Walker; p.63 (a) ©Bob Daemmrich/Stock Boston; p.63 (b) Park Street; p.63 (c) Ken Lax C; p.63 (d) Tomás Ovalle; p.64 (a) Ken Walker; p.64 (b) Dan Cohen; p.64 (c) Christine Galida; pp.64 (d), 65 (c) Park Street; p.65 (d) Rick Williams; p.65 (f) Ken Walker; p.67 Park Street; p.68 Rick Williams; p.69 Christina Galida; p.70 ©Bob Daemmrich/Stock Boston; p.71 ©David J Sams/Stone; p.72 (a) ©Superstock; p.72 (b) Park Street; p.72 (c) Christine Galida; p.72 (d) Rick Williams; p.74 (a, c) Ken Walker; p.74 (b) Ken Lax; p.74 (d) Christina Galida; p.75 (a) Ken Lax; p.75 (b, c) Christina Galida; p.75 (d) Park Street; p.76 (a) Dan Cohen; p.76 (b, d) Ken Lax; p.76 (c) Ken Walker; p.77 (a, c) Christina Galida; p.77 (b) Dan Cohen; p.77 (d) Rick Williams; p.78 (a, b) Park Street; p.78 (c, d) Christina Galida; p.79 (a) Dan Cohen; p.79 (b, d) Christine Galida; p.79 (c) Jeff Gritchen; p.81 Rick Williams; p.83 Dan Cohen; p.84 Christine Galida; p.85 Park Street; p.86 (a) Christine Galida; p.86 (b) Dan Cohen; p.88 (a, b) Jeff Gritchen; p.88 (d) Ken Lax; p.89 (a) Tomás Ovalle; p.89 (b, c) Park Street; pp.89 (d), 90 (a, c) Dan Cohen; p.90 (b) Rick Williams; pp.90 (d), 91 (a, c) Tomás Ovalle; p.91 (b) Dan Cohen; p.92 Park Street; p.93 Dan Cohen; p.94 ©Hans Reinhard/Stone; p.95 (b) Ken Lax; p.95 (d) Christine Galida; p.101 (b) Ken Walker; p.105 Tomás Ovalle; p.106 Ken Lax.

ISBN 0-7398-2839-8

Printed in the United States of America
13 14 15 16 2266 15 14 13 12
4500395944

Contents

To the Learner

You are starting *Book One* in the *Reading for Today* series. This book begins by reviewing the sounds the letters stand for. Since these sounds are also presented in the *Introductory Book*, you can go first to that book if you prefer a whole page of practice on each sound.

Also in *Book One*, you will learn 120 sight words. These are the most common words that occur in writing. As you learn new words, please write them in a journal or notebook. You'll work on exercises to strengthen your vocabulary and comprehension skills. You will also learn to use context clues and your own experience to help you understand what you read. And you will think, discuss, and write, all of which are part of reading in today's world.

Your reading skills are getting stronger every day. Think about how reading can help you meet a goal you have set for yourself in daily life or on the job. List one or two goals you have set for yourself.

Instructor's Notes: Read this page to students, flip through the pages, and discuss the phonics and sight word lessons to come. Point out that students will be reading sentences by page 12 and paragraphs by page 24. Refer to the *Reading for Today Instructor's Guide* for the answer key, lesson plans, blackline masters, and a discussion of how to use the Learner Placement Form on the inside back cover of this book. Note the writing icon beginning on page 8 and tell students it indicates a place for them to produce their own writing. If in the next few pages students have difficulty identifying consonant sounds, use Blackline Master 2 in the *Reading for Today Instructor's Guide* for additional practice.

Unit 1 Reviewing Consonant Sounds

Review b, c, d, f

A. Write b, c, d, or f.

1.

_d_ og

2.

___ee

3.

lea___

4.

___at

5.

___ork

6.

tu___

7.

___up

8.

foo___

9.

___ar

10.

we___

11.

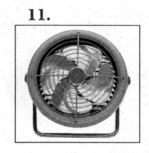

___an

12.

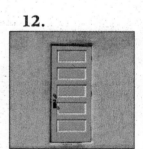

___oor

B. Write two words that begin with b or c.

_____   _____

C. Write two words that begin with d or f.

_____   _____

Instructor's Notes: Review these consonant sounds: *b* in *bee*, *c* in *cat*, *d* in *dog*, and *f* in *fork*. The sounds occur at both the beginning and end of words. Review the picture names: 1 dog, 2 bee, 3 leaf, 4 cat, 5 fork, 6 tub, 7 cup, 8 food, 9 car, 10 web, 11 fan, 12 door. For A, have students say each picture name before writing letters. For B and C, students may pick words from A or write others.

1

Unit 1

Review g, h, j, k

A. Write g, h, j, or k.

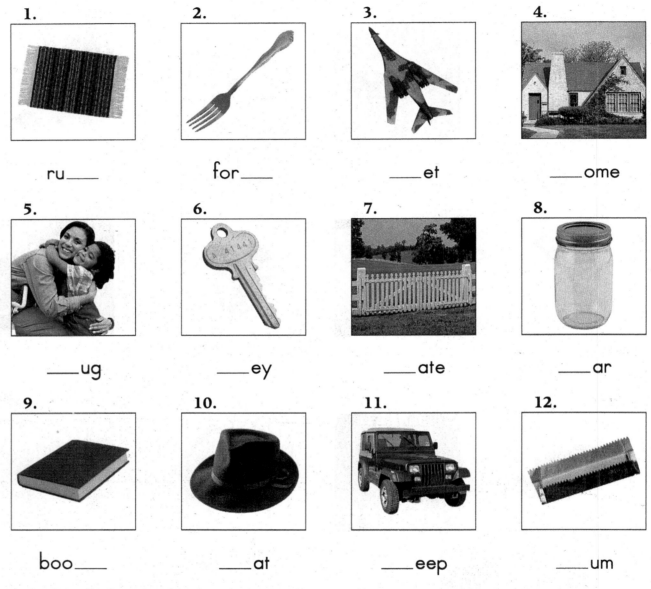

1. ru____

2. for____

3. ____et

4. ____ome

5. ____ug

6. ____ey

7. ____ate

8. ____ar

9. boo____

10. ____at

11. ____eep

12. ____um

B. Write two words that begin with g or h.

_____   _____

C. Write two words that begin with j or k.

_____   _____

Instructor's Notes: Review these consonant sounds: g in gate, h in home, j in jar, and k in key. The sounds occur at both the beginning and end of words. Review the picture names: 1 rug, 2 fork, 3 jet, 4 home, 5 hug, 6 key, 7 gate, 8 jar, 9 book, 10 hat, 11 jeep, 12 gum. For A, have students say each picture name before writing letters. For B and C, students may pick words from A or write others.

Review l, m, n, p

A. Write l, m, n, or p.

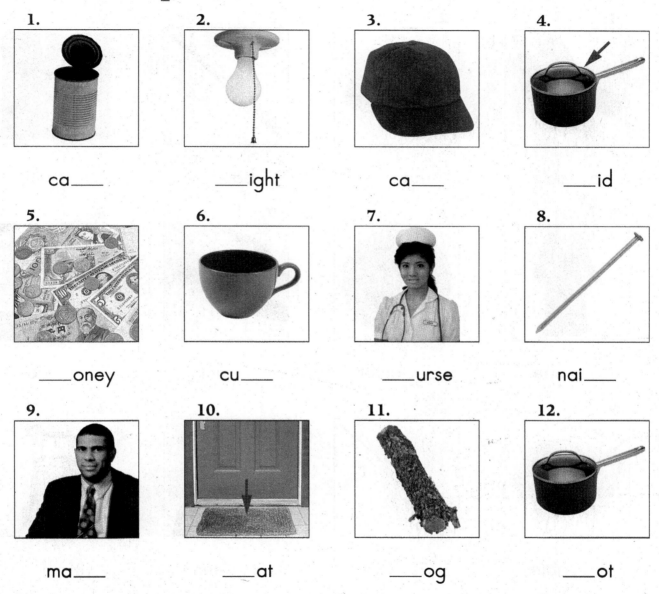

1. ca___

2. ___ight

3. ca___

4. ___id

5. ___oney

6. cu___

7. ___urse

8. nai___

9. ma___

10. ___at

11. ___og

12. ___ot

B. Write two words that begin with l or m.

_____   _____

C. Write two words that begin with n or p.

_____   _____

Instructor's Notes: Review these consonant sounds: *l* in *light*, *m* in *moon*, *n* in *nurse*, and *p* in *pot*. The sounds occur at both the beginning and end of words. Review the picture names: 1 can, 2 light, 3 cap, 4 lid, 5 money, 6 cup, 7 nurse, 8 nail, 9 man, 10 mat, 11 log, 12 pot. For A, have students say each picture name before writing letters. For B and C, students may pick words from A or write others.

Review qu, r, s, t

A. Write qu, r, s, or t.

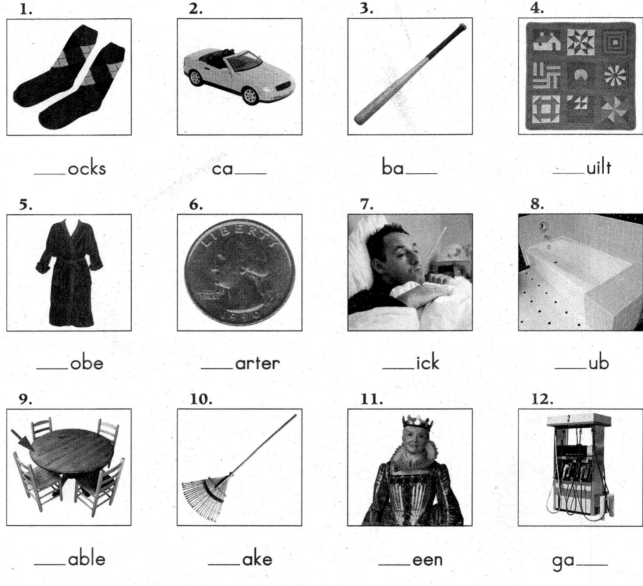

1.

____ocks

2.

ca____

3.

ba____

4.

____uilt

5.

____obe

6.

____arter

7.

____ick

8.

____ub

9.

____able

10.

____ake

11.

____een

12.

ga____

B. Write two words that begin with qu or r.

_____   _____

C. Write two words that begin with s or t.

_____   _____

Instructor's Notes: Review these consonant sounds: *qu* in *quilt*, *r* in *robe*, *s* in *socks*, and *t* in *tiger.* Point out that *u* is always used with *q*. The sounds occur at both the beginning and end of words, except *qu*. Review the picture names: 1 socks, 2 car, 3 bat, 4 quilt, 5 robe, 6 quarter, 7 sick, 8 tub, 9 table, 10 rake, 11 queen, 12 gas. For A, have students say each picture name before writing letters.

Review v, w, x, y, z

A. Write v, w, x, y, or z.

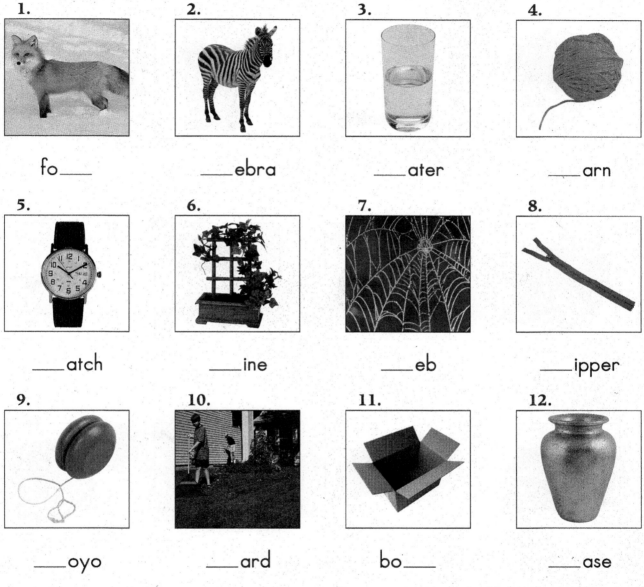

1. fo___

2. ___ebra

3. ___ater

4. ___arn

5. ___atch

6. ___ine

7. ___eb

8. ___ipper

9. ___oyo

10. ___ard

11. bo___

12. ___ase

B. Write two words that begin with v or w.

_____   _____

C. Write two words that begin with x, y, or z.

_____   _____

Instructor's Notes: Review these consonant sounds: v in *vase*, w in *web*, x in *fox*, y in *yell*, and z in *zebra*. The sounds occur at both the beginning and end of words. Review the picture names: 1 fox, 2 zebra, 3 water, 4 yarn, 5 watch, 6 vine, 7 web, 8 zipper, 9 yoyo 10 yard, 11 box, 12 vase. For A, have students say each picture name before writing letters. Then assign *Reading for Today Workbook One*, Unit 1.

Review   Short <u>a</u>

A. Write the missing letters.

1.

____pple

2.

c____t

3.

j____m

4.

m____t

5.
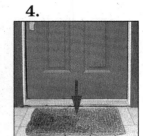
c____p

6.

p____n

7.

c____n

8.

____nt

9.

v____n

10.

m____p

11.

b____t

12.

h____t

B. Write two words with the short <u>a</u> sound.

_____   _____

Instructor's Notes: Read the directions and review the picture names: 1 apple, 2 cat, 3 jam, 4 mat, 5 cap, 6 pan, 7 can, 8 ant, 9 van, 10 map, 11 bat, 12 hat. For A, use *cat* and *jam* to point out the consonant-short vowel-consonant (CVC) pattern. Use *apple* and *ant* to point out that vowels can also begin words. For B, students may pick words from A or write others.

Review Long a

A. Write the missing letters.

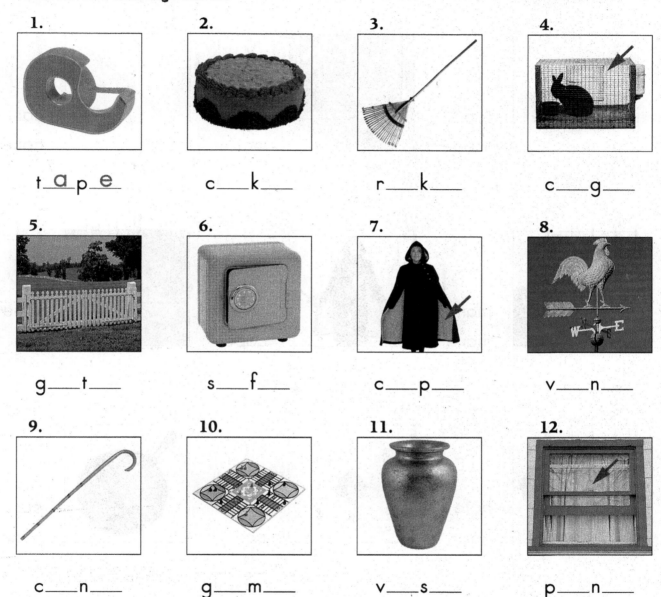

1. t <u>a p e</u>

2. c__k__

3. r__k__

4. c__g__

5. g__t__

6. s__f__

7. c__p__

8. v__n__

9. c__n__

10. g__m__

11. v__s__

12. p__n__

B. Write two words with the long a sound.

_____   _____

Instructor's Notes: Read the directions and review the picture names: 1 tape, 2 cake, 3 rake, 4 cage, 5 gate, 6 safe, 7 cape, 8 vane, 9 cane, 10 game, 11 vase, 12 pane. For A, use *tape* and *cake* to point out the consonant–long vowel–consonant + silent *e* (CVC + *e*) pattern. For B, students may pick words from A or write others.

Review Long a and Short a

A. Circle the word. Write the word.

1.

tap
(tape)

tape

2.

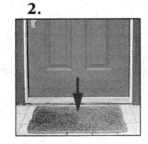

mate
mat

_____

3.

can
cane

_____

4.

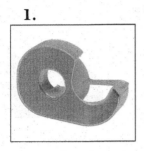

man
mane

_____

5.

cap
cape

_____

6.

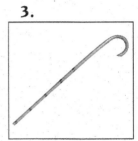

vane
van

_____

7.

hate
hat

_____

8.

am
ace

_____

9.

pan
pane

_____

 B. Write a sentence with a long a word.

_____

 C. Write a sentence with a short a word.

_____

Instructor's Notes: Review the picture names and word choices: 1 tape, 2 mat, 3 cane, 4 man, 5 cape, 6 vane, 7 hat, 8 ace, 9 pan. For A, use *tap* and *tape* to review the difference between the CVC and the CVC + e pattern. For B and C, have students use words from A to dictate a sentence. Write the sentence and have students copy it or help students write the sentence.

Review Short i

A. Write the missing letters.

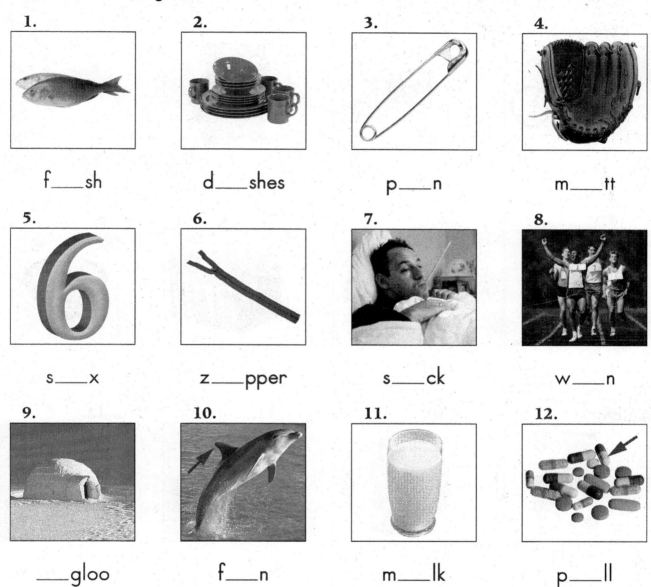

1.

f___sh

2.

d___shes

3.

p___n

4.

m___tt

5.

s___x

6.

z___pper

7.

s___ck

8.

w___n

9.

___gloo

10.

f___n

11.

m___lk

12.

p___ll

B. Write two words with the short i sound.

_____   _____

Instructor's Notes: Read the directions and review the picture names: 1 fish, 2 dishes, 3 pin, 4 mitt, 5 six , 6 zipper, 7 sick, 8 win, 9 igloo, 10 fin, 11 milk, 12 pill. For A, use *fish* and *pin* to point out the consonant-short vowel-consonant (CVC) pattern Use *fish* and *mitt* to point out that some words end in two consonants. For B, students may pick words from A or write others.

9

Unit 2

Review Long i

A. Write the missing letters.

1. 
b__k__

2. 
p__n__

3. 
v__n__

4. 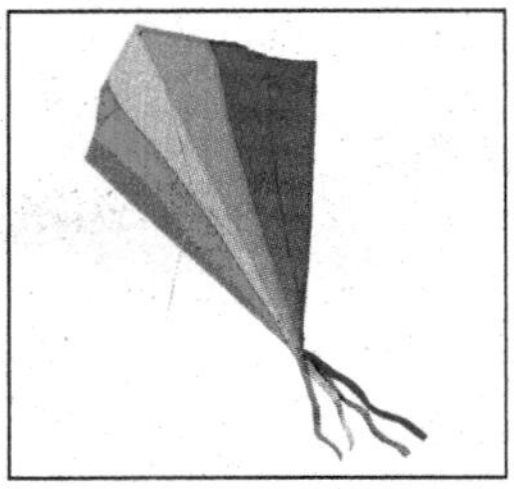
k__t__

5. 
h__v__

6. 
d__c__

7. 
f__l__

8. 
r__c__

9. 
f__v__

10. 
d__m__

11. 
m__c__

12. 
r__d__

B. Write two words with the long i sound.

_____   _____

Instructor's Notes: Read the directions and review the picture names: 1 bike, 2 pine, 3 vine, 4 kite, 5 hive, 6 dice, 7 file, 8 rice, 9 five, 10 dime, 11 mice, 12 ride. For A, use *bike* and *pine* to point out the CVC + *e* pattern. For B, students may pick words from A or write others.

Review Long i and Short i

A. Circle the word. Write the word.

1.

pine
pin

_____

2.

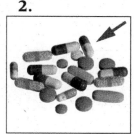

pile
pill

_____

3.

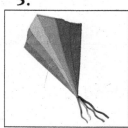

kit
kite

_____

4.

win
wine

_____

5.

fill
file

_____

6.

fin
fine

_____

7.

dim
dime

_____

8.

Tim
time

_____

9.

ride
rid

_____

B. Write a sentence with a long i word.

_____

C. Write a sentence with a short i word.

_____

Instructor's Notes: Review the picture names and word choices: 1 pine, 2 pill 3, kite, 4 win, 5 file, 6 fin, 7 dime, 8 time, 9 ride. For A, use *pin* and *pine* to review the difference between the CVC and the CVC + *e* pattern. For B and C, have students use words from A to dictate a sentence. Write the sentence and have students copy it or help students write the sentence.

11

Unit 2

Read each sentence. Circle the missing word. Write the word.

1. One day we flew a _____ .

   kite
   bite
   kit

   _____

2. It landed in a _____ tree.

   pin
   gate
   pine

   _____

3. The kite hit a bee _____ in the tree.

   dive
   hive
   five

   _____

4. The bees _____ at us so we ran.

   tame
   same
   came

   _____

5. We had to _____ away from the bees.

   race
   pace
   rate

   _____

6. We ran away just in _____ .

   Tim
   time
   tide

Think About It

1. What did they fly?
2. What did it hit?
3. Did the bees get them?

Instructor's Notes: Review these sight words: *one*, *day*, *flew*, *a*, *the*, *so*, *from*. Read the story with students. Review the choices for each blank before picking the correct word. Read the questions together and discuss the answers.

Review Short o

A. Write the missing letters.

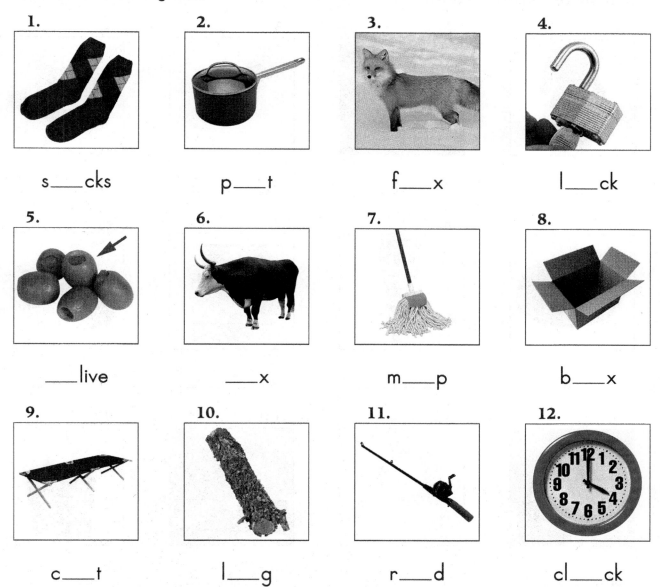

1.

s___cks

2.

p___t

3.

f___x

4.

l___ck

5.

___live

6.

___x

7.

m___p

8.

b___x

9.

c___t

10.

l___g

11.

r___d

12.

cl___ck

B. Write two words with the short o sound.

_____   _____

Instructor's Notes: Read the directions and review the picture names: 1 socks, 2 pot, 3 fox, 4 lock, 5 olive, 6 ox, 7 mop, 8 box, 9 cot, 10 log, 11 rod, 12 clock. For A, use *pot* and *fox* to point out the consonant-short vowel-consonant (CVC) pattern. Use *clock* to point out that some words begin or end with more than one consonant. Use *olive* to point out that some words begin with vowels. For B, students may pick words from A or write others.

Review Long <u>o</u>

A. Write the missing letters.

1.

r__b___

2.

h__l___

3.

b__n___

4.

n__t___

5.

h__s___

6.

c__n___

7.
st__v___

8.
r__s___

9.
sm__k___

10.
r__p___

11.
h__m___

12.
t__t___

B. Write two words with the long <u>o</u> sound.

_____   _____

Instructor's Notes: Read the directions and review the picture names: 1 robe, 2 hole, 3 bone, 4 note, 5 hose, 6 cone, 7 stove, 8 rose, 9 smoke, 10 rope, 11 home, 12 tote. For A, use *robe* and *hole* to point out the CVC + *e* pattern. For B, students may pick words from A or write others.

Review   Long o and Short o

A. Circle the word. Write the word.

1.

rob
robe

_____

2.

mope
mop

_____

3.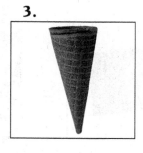

con
cone

_____

4.

rope
rod

_____

5.

dog
dome

_____

6.

tot
tote

_____

7.

lock
lone

_____

8.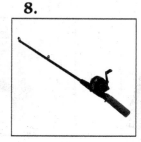

rode
rod

_____

9.

not
note

_____

 B. Write a sentence with a long o word.

_____

 C. Write a sentence with a short o word.

_____

Instructor's Notes: Review the picture names and word choices: 1 robe, 2 mop, 3 cone, 4 rope, 5 dog, 6 tote, 7 lock, 8 rod, 9 note. For A, use *rob* and *robe* to review the difference between the CVC and the CVC + *e* pattern. For B and C, have students use words from A to dictate a sentence. Write the sentence and have students copy it or help students write the sentence.

15

Unit 2

Review Short <u>u</u>

A. Write the missing letters.

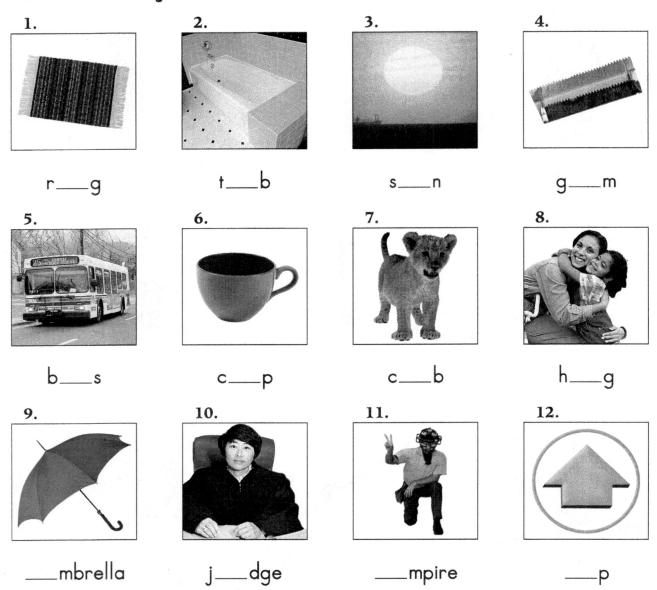

1. r__g

2. t__b

3. s__n

4. g__m

5. b__s

6. c__p

7. c__b

8. h__g

9. __mbrella

10. j__dge

11. __mpire

12. __p

B. Write two words with the short <u>u</u> sound.

_____   _____

Instructor's Notes: Read the directions and review the picture names: 1 rug, 2 tub, 3 sun, 4 gum, 5 bus, 6 cup, 7 cub, 8 hug, 9 umbrella, 10 judge, 11 umpire, 12 up. For A, use *rug* and *tub* to point out the consonant-short vowel-consonant (CVC) pattern. For B, the student may pick words from A or write others.

Review Long u

A. Write the missing letters.

1.

m___l___

2.

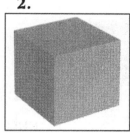

c___b___

3.

f___s___

4.

t___b___

5.

J___n___

6.

fl___t___

7.

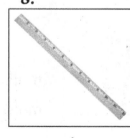

t___n___

8.

r___l___r

9.

f___m___s

B. Write two words with the long u sound.

_____   _____

Instructor's Notes: Read the directions and review the picture names: 1 mule, 2 cube, 3 fuse, 4 tube, 5 June, 6 flute, 7 tune, 8 ruler, 9 fumes. For A, use *mule* and *cube* to point out the CVC + *e* pattern. Some students may hear the difference in the long *u* sound in *mule* and *tune*. The sounds are different, but both are generally called long *u*.

Review Long u and Short u

A. Circle the word. Write the word.

1.

tube
tub

_____

2.

cube
cub

_____

3.

fuss
fuse

_____

4.

tube
tub

_____

5.
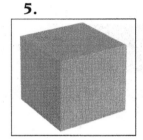
cube
cub

_____

6.

hug
huge

_____

7.
music staff
tan
tune

_____

8.

mull
mule

_____

9.

cut
cute

_____

 B. Write a sentence with a long u word.

_____

 C. Write a sentence with a short u word.

_____

Instructor's Notes: Review the picture names and word choices: 1 tube, 2 cub, 3 fuse, 4 tub, 5 cube, 6 hug, 7 tune, 8 mule, 9 cut. For A, use *tub* and *tube* to review the difference between the CVC and the CVC + *e* pattern. For B and C, have students use words from A to dictate a sentence. Write the sentence and have students copy it or help students write the sentence.

Read a Story

Read each pair of sentences. Circle the missing words. Write the words.

1. How can you get a _____ to move?

rule
mule
mole

2. You can pull it by the _____ .

hose
rose
nose

_____

3. What can you do if the lights go out at _____ ?

bone
home
him

4. You can check the _____ box.

hose
fuse
fuss

_____

5. Why does a dog dig a _____ ?

pole
role
hole

6. A dog digs to hide a _____ .

tone
bone
lone

Instructor's Notes: Review these sight words: *how, you, to, move, the, what, do, lights, go, out, why, does, a.* Read each question and answer together. Have students think about which word choice makes the most sense in each sentence. Discuss the answers.

19

Unit 2

Review   Short e

A. Write the missing letters.

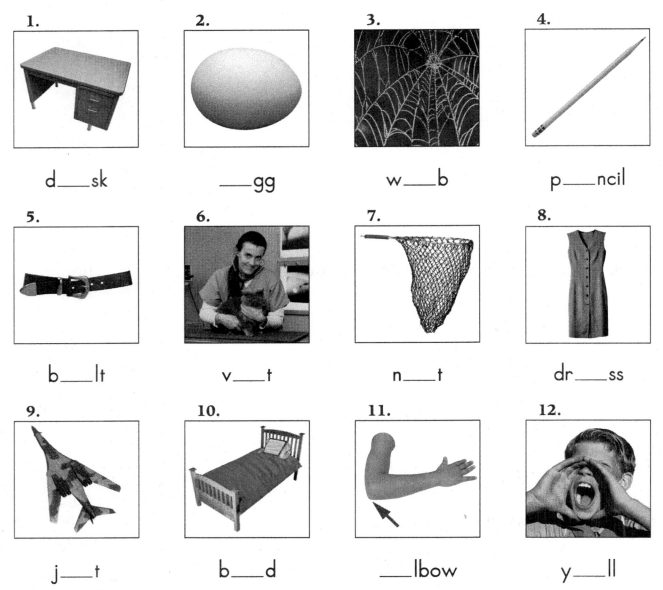

1.
d___sk

2.
___gg

3.
w___b

4.
p___ncil

5.
b___lt

6.
v___t

7.
n___t

8.
dr___ss

9.
j___t

10.
b___d

11.
___lbow

12.
y___ll

B. Write two words with the short e sound.

_____   _____

Instructor's Notes: Read the directions and review the picture names: 1 desk, 2 egg, 3 web, 4 pencil, 5 belt, 6 vet, 7 net, 8 dress, 9 jet, 10 bed, 11 elbow, 12 yell. For A, use *web* and *pencil* to point out the consonant-short vowel-consonant (CVC) pattern. Use *desk* to point out that some words end with two consonants. Use *egg* to point out that some words begin with vowels.

Review Long e

A. Write the missing letter.

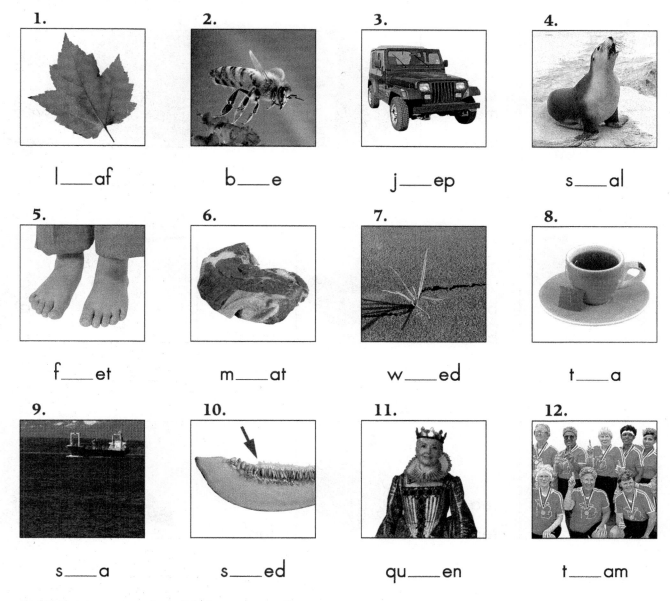

1. l___af

2. b___e

3. j___ep

4. s___al

5. f___et

6. m___at

7. w___ed

8. t___a

9. s___a

10. s___ed

11. qu___en

12. t___am

B. Write two words with long vowel ea.

_____   _____

C. Write two words with long vowel ee.

_____   _____

Instructor's Notes: Read the directions and review the picture names: 1 leaf, 2 bee, 3 jeep, 4 seal, 5 feet, 6 meat, 7 weed, 8 tea, 9 sea, 10 seed 11 queen, 12 team. For A, use *leaf* and *bee* to point out the long *e* vowel sound that can be spelled *ee* or *ea*. For B, students may pick words from A or write others.

Review Long e and Short e

A. Circle the word. Write the word.

1.
mean
men

_____

2.
sell
seal

_____

3.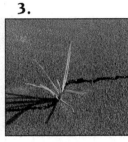
wed
weed

_____

4.
bead
bed

_____

5.
met
meat

_____

6.
neat
net

_____

7.
tea
ten

_____

8.
left
leaf

_____

9.
beet
bet

_____

B. Write a sentence with a long e word.

_____

C. Write a sentence with a short e word.

_____

Instructor's Notes: Review the picture names and word choices: 1 men, 2 seal, 3 weed, 4 bed, 5 meat, 6 net, 7 tea, 8 leaf, 9 beet. Use *men* and *mean* to review the difference between short e words and long *ea*, *ee* words. For B and C, have students use words from A to dictate a sentence. Write the sentence and have students copy it or help students write the sentence.

22

Read a Story

Read each sentence. Circle the missing word. Write the word.

1. I went to the baseball game with _____ .

Ted
Cub
Get

_____

2. We _____ the bus to the game.

hole
rule
rode

_____

3. We had good _____ at the game.

beaks
weeks
seats

_____

4. I had a hot dog to _____ .

beep
eat
beat

_____

5. Sue had an ice-cream _____ .

tone
cone
bone

_____

6. The _____ that won the game was the Red Sox.

seem
team
beam

Think About It

1. How did they get to the game?
2. What did they eat?
3. Who was the team that won?
4. Tell about a game you have seen.

Instructor's Notes: Review these sight words: *baseball*, *the*, *to*, *good*, *a*, *an*, *was*, *that*. Read the story with students. Review the answer choices together before students pick the correct word. Read the questions together and discuss the answers. Then assign *Reading for Today Workbook One*, Unit 2.

23

Unit 2

big ● man ● run ● sit ● stand

A. Read the new words above with your teacher.

B. Look at the picture. Read each word.

C. Listen to your teacher read the story. Try to read it as you listen. Then circle the new words from the picture. Read each word.

It is the end of the big race.

A man and a woman stand.

A boy and a girl sit.

Two people run to win the race.

Who will win the race?

Instructor's Notes: Introduce the new words at the top of the page. Students may recognize some words, such as *man*, from Units 1 and 2; however these words are treated as "new" in Unit 3 to make sure students know them in sentence context. Discuss the picture and have students predict what the story is about; discuss predictions later. Read the story aloud and ask students to circle the new words.

Writing Skills

A. Read the new words on page 24. Use the picture to help you.

B. Write the missing letter in each new word. Then write the word below.

1. __b__ ig

_____big_____

2. ru____

_____

3. si____

_____

4. m____n

_____

5. st____nd

_____

C. Write the new word that goes with each picture.

1. ____man____

2. _____

3. _____

4. _____

5. _____

Instructor's Notes: Read the five new words and have students repeat after you. Then read the directions together. Have students make flash cards to practice the new words. Have students think of words that mean the opposite of *big (little)* and *sit (stand)*.

Sight Words

can ● go ● stop
food ● table

A. Read the new words above with your teacher.

B. Look at the picture. Read each word.

C. Listen to your teacher read the story. Try to read it as you listen. Then circle the new words from the picture. Read each word.

A man and a woman stop at the store.

They go into the store.

He buys a can of food.

She buys some food for lunch.

They stand next to a table.

Instructor's Notes: Introduce new words. Discuss the picture and have students predict what the story is about; discuss predictions later. Read the story aloud and ask students to circle the new words. Have them think of words that mean the opposite of *stop (go)* and *can (cannot)*.

A. Read the words on page 26. Use the picture to help you.

B. Write the missing letter or letters in each new word. Then write the word below.

1. c_a_n

_____

2. t____ble

_____

3. st____p

_____

4. g____

_____

5. f____ ____d

_____

C. Listen to your teacher read each sentence. Then write the missing word.

1. She opens a _____can_____ of beans for lunch.

2. He opens a can of cat _____ for the cat.

3. They sit at the _____ to eat lunch.

4. I _____ the car at a red light.

5. I look before I _____ when the light is green.

D. Write a sentence for each of the new words. Your teacher will help with your sentences.

1. _____

2. _____

3. _____

4. _____

5. _____

Instructor's Notes: For A, read the five new words and have students repeat. Then read the directions together. For C, read each sentence to students. For D, help as needed.

27

Unit 3

Writing Skills

Adding -s and -es
to Action Words

A. Add -s or -es to each word. Then write the new word.

1. run   + **s**   = run **s**   _____ runs _____

2. go   + **es** = go____   _____

3. sit   + **s**   = sit____   _____

4. do   + **es** = do____   _____

5. stand + **s**   = stand____   _____

6. watch + **es** = watch____   _____

7. stop   + **s**   = stop____   _____

8. fix   + **es** = fix____   _____

B. Read these sentences. Then underline the one that goes with the picture.

1. A man runs.

2. A man stops.

3. A man stands.

4. A man sits.

Instructor's Notes: Write and read to the student: *He runs. She runs.* Ask which letter was added to run *(s)*. Write and read to the student: *He goes. She goes.* Ask which letters were added to go *(es)*.

28

Unit 3

C. **Add -s or -es to each of the action words in the story below.**

1. Hector go __es__ to the store.

2. He stop____ by the bell peppers.

3. Hector often fix____ pizza.

4. Amalia watch____ him roll the crust.

5. Finally the family sit____ down to eat.

6. Amalia do____ the dishes.

D. **Write the word that goes with each picture.**

fixes   stands   watches   sits   goes   runs

1.

__runs__

2.

_____

3.

_____

4.

_____

5.

_____

6.

_____

Instructor's Notes: For C, read the words from A on page 28. Then read the sentences with students. For D, read the directions and the words with students.

A. Look at each picture. Then read the words. Write the word that goes with the picture.

1._____
   stand   can

2._____
   go   sit

3._____
   food   table

4._____
   run   stop

B. Look at each picture. Underline the sentence that goes with the picture. Write the sentence.

<u>A man sits.</u>
A man stands.

A man runs.
A man stops.

The dog is big.
The man is big.

1. ___A man sits.___

2. _____

3. _____

Instructor's Notes: Review the ten sight words from pages 24–27. Have the student make up a sentence for each word. For A and B, read the directions to the student and discuss the pictures. For B, discuss the completed first item.

30

Unit 3

A woman can lift.
A woman watches.

A man goes.
A man fixes.

A girl runs.
A girl does homework.

4. _____

5. _____

6. _____

C. Read these sentences. Then underline the one that goes with the picture.

1. The woman goes.

2. The woman fixes.

3. The woman watches.

4. The woman does.

D. Add -s or -es to each word. Then write the new word.

1. do   + **es** = do____   _____

2. stop   + **s**   = stop____   _____

3. fix   + **es** = fix____   _____

4. stand + **s**   = stand____   _____

Instructor's Notes: Review the ten sight words from pages 24–27. For C, discuss the picture and have the student say all the sentences before picking the right one. For D, have the student say each word before writing the word.

A. Read the new words above with your teacher.

B. Look at the picture. Read each word.

**C. Listen to your teacher read the story. Try to read it as you listen.
Then circle the new words from the picture. Read each word.**

The woman is home from her job.

She will use her key to open the door.

She waves at a friend.

He is going for a walk.

Instructor's Notes: Introduce new words. Discuss the picture and have students predict what the story is about; discuss predictions later. Read the story aloud and ask students to circle the new words. Have them think of words that mean the opposite of *walk (run)* and *woman (man)*.

A. Read the words on page 32. Use the picture to help you.

B. Write the missing letter for each word. Then write the word below.

1. hom____

_____

2. wa____k

_____

3. ke____

_____

4. us____

_____

5. w____man

_____

C. Listen to your teacher say each sentence. Then write the missing new word.

1. This _____ will open the car door.

2. The _____ found her car key.

3. She will go _____ after work.

4. Did he _____ to the bus stop?

5. I _____ a bus to get to work.

D. Write a sentence for each of the new words. Your teacher will help with your sentences.

1. _____

2. _____

3. _____

4. _____

5. _____

Instructor's Notes: For A, read the five new words and have students repeat them. Then read the directions for B together. For C, read each sentence to students. For D, help as needed.

**buy ● dog ● money
radio ● yell**

A. Read the new words above with your teacher.

B. Look at the picture. Read each word.

**C. Listen to your teacher read the story. Try to read it as you listen.
Then circle the new words from the picture. Read each word.**

The woman has some money.

She wants to buy the radio.

The man has to yell at his dog.

He tells the dog to stop barking.

Instructor's Notes: Introduce new words. Discuss the picture and have students predict what
the story is about; discuss predictions later. Read the story aloud and ask students to circle the
new words. Have them think of words that mean the opposite of *buy (sell)* and *yell (whisper)*.

A. Read the new words on page 34. Use the picture to help you.

B. Write the missing letters in each new word. Then write the word below.

1. y__ __ __

_____

2. __o__

_____

3. r__ __ __ __

_____

4. b__ __

_____

5. m__ __ __ __

_____

C. Write the new word that goes with each picture.

1. _____

2. _____

3. _____

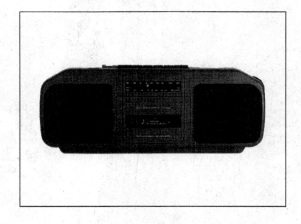

4. _____

5. _____

Instructor's Notes: Read the five new words and have students repeat after you. Then read the directions together. Have students make flash cards to practice the new words.

35

Unit 3

Adding -s and -es
to Naming Words

A. Add -s or -es to each word. Then write the new word.

1. home + **s** = home____   _____

2. ranch + **es** = ranch____   _____

3. key + **s** = key____   _____

4. grass + **es** = grass____   _____

5. dog + **s** = dog____   _____

6. boss + **es** = boss____   _____

7. table + **s** = table____   _____

8. box + **es** = box____   _____

9. radio + **s** = radio____   _____

B. Read these sentences. Then underline the one that goes with the picture.

1. A man uses keys.

2. The man buys radios.

3. The woman buys tables.

4. A woman stops the dogs.

5. The dogs run.

Instructor's Notes: Write and read to students: *homes.* Ask which letter was added to *home (s).*
Write and read to students: *ranches.* Ask which letters were added to *ranch (es).* For A and B,
read the directions and discuss the first item together.

C. Write the word that goes with each picture.

homes   dogs   radios   grasses   boxes   keys   tables   bosses

1. _____

2. _____

3. _____

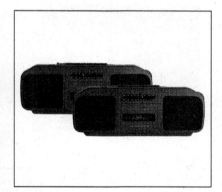

4. _____

5. _____

6. _____

7. _____

8. _____

Instructor's Notes: For C, read the directions and the words with students.

Review Pages 32–37

A. Look at each picture. Then read the sentences. Write the word that goes with each picture.

1. The man uses _____ .
              key   money

2. A _____ walks home.
        woman   radio

4. The man

_____
    uses   yells

3. The woman _____ .
         buys   yells

a radio.

B. Look at each picture. Then read the sentences. Underline the one that goes with the picture. Then write the sentence.

A man buys dogs.
A man buys radios.

The dogs sit.
The dogs walk.

1. _____

2. _____

Instructor's Notes: Review the ten sight words from pages 32–35. Have students make up a sentence for each word. For A and B, read the directions to students and discuss the pictures.

38

Unit 3

A woman uses keys.
A woman uses money.

The man yells.
The man walks.

3. _____

4. _____

The tables sit on the grass.
The boys sit on the grass.

The woman carries boxes.
The woman carries radios.

5. _____

6. _____

C. Read the sentences. Then underline the one that goes with the picture.

1. The woman uses money.

2. The woman walks the dogs.

3. The man buys radios.

4. The man yells at the dogs.

5. The keys are on the table.

Instructor's Notes: Review the ten sight words from pages 32-35. For C, discuss the picture and have the student say all the sentences before picking the right one.

brother ● car ● country
sister ● work

A. Read the new words above with your teacher.

B. Look at the picture. Read each word.

C. Listen to your teacher read the story. Try to read it as you listen. Then circle the new words from the picture. Read each word.

The car is on the country road.

The man is starting to work on it.

His brother and sister watch him work.

They want to go for a ride.

Instructor's Notes: Introduce the new words. Discuss the picture and have students predict what the story is about; discuss predictions later. Read the story aloud and ask students to circle the new words. Have them think of words that mean the opposite of *brother (sister)* and *work (play)*.

A. Read the words on page 40. Use the picture to help you.

B. Write the missing letters in these words. Then write the words.

1. broth____ ____

2. c____ ____

3. sist____ ____

_____

_____

_____

4. w____ ____k

5. count____ ____

_____

_____

C. Listen to your teacher read each sentence. Then write the missing word.

1. The man can _____ on the car.

2. He likes to go fishing in the _____ .

3. He has a big _____ .

4. Jim is his little _____ .

5. Ann is his little _____ .

D. Write a sentence for each of the new words. Your teacher will help with the other words.

1. _____

2. _____

3. _____

4. _____

5. _____

Instructor's Notes: For A, read the five new words and have students repeat them. Then read the directions for B together. For C, read each sentence to students. For D, help as needed.

41

Unit 3

Sight Words   family ● van ● look
help ● water

A. Read the new words above with your teacher.

B. Look at the picture. Read each word.

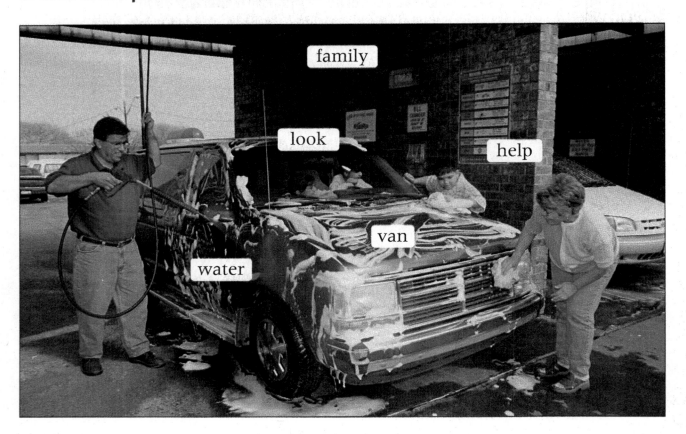

**C. Listen to your teacher read the story. Try to read it as you listen.
Then circle the new words from the picture. Read each word.**

The family is washing the van.

Dad sprays on the water.

Mom washes the van with the soap.

The son will help dry the van.

His little sisters play in the van.

They look out the window.

Instructor's Notes: Introduce the new words. Discuss the picture and have students predict what the story is about; discuss predictions later. Read the story aloud and ask students to circle the new words.

A. Read the new words on page 42. Use the picture to help you.

B. Write the missing letters in each new word. Then write the words.

1. f___m___ly

2. loo___

3. v___ ___

_____

_____

_____

4. wa___e___

5. h___l___

_____

_____

C. Listen to your teacher read each sentence. Then write the missing word.

1. Ted has two little sisters in his _____ .

2. Ted likes to _____ out for his little sisters.

3. The family all ride in the _____ .

4. They wash the van with soap and _____ .

5. The sisters want to _____ wash the van.

D. Write a sentence with each of the new words. Your teacher will help with the other words.

1. _____

2. _____

3. _____

4. _____

5. _____

Instructor's Notes: For A, read the five new words and have students repeat them. Then read the directions for B together. For C, read each sentence to students. For D, help as needed.

43

Unit 3

Writing Skills

Adding -ed
to Action Words

A. Add -ed to each word. Then write the new word.

1. work + **ed** = work____   _____

2. help   + **ed** = help____   _____

3. look   + **ed** = look____   _____

4. yell   + **ed** = yell____   _____

5. walk + **ed** = walk____   _____

B. Read these sentences. Then underline the one that goes with the picture.

1. The people worked.

2. A dog walked.

3. A man walked.

4. The sister yelled.

5. The woman helped.

Instructor's Notes: To introduce the concept of adding *-ed* to verbs to form the past tense, write and read to students: *I work. I worked.* Ask what was added to *work (ed)*. Discuss the meaning of past time. For A and B, read the directions together and help students complete the activities.

44

Unit 3

C. Look at each picture. Then read the sentences. Write the word that best completes each sentence.

1.

walked
yelled

She _____ home.

2.

looked
worked

He _____ at the store.

3.

helped
worked

She _____ with dinner.

4.

helped
yelled

He _____ at the dog.

5.

looked
walked

She _____ at the game.

D. Look at each picture. Then read the sentences. Underline the one that goes with the picture.

1.

The brother yelled.
The brother walked.

2.

He walked home.
He helped fix the pipe.

3.

The woman yelled.
The woman worked.

Instructor's Notes: For C, read the sight words and directions together. For D, read the directions to students and discuss the pictures.

A. Look at each picture. Then read the sentences. Write the word that goes with each picture.

1. This is a _____ home.
      food   country

2. The _____ runs.
      van   look

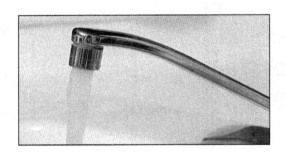

3. The cars _____ .
      go   table

4. The _____ runs.
      water   country

B. Look at each picture. Then read the sentences. Underline the one that goes with the picture. Then write the sentence.

The sister worked.
The car worked.

The water helped.
The brother helped.

The family looked.
The family yelled.

1. _____   **2.** _____   **3.** _____

Instructor's Notes: Review the ten sight words from pages 40–43. Have students make up a sentence for each word. For A and B, read the directions to students and discuss the pictures.

46

Unit 3

The dog walked.
The family walked.

The sister yelled.
The family yelled.

The water worked.
The brother worked.

4. _____

5. _____

6. _____

C. Read the words. Then read the sentence. Write the word that best completes each sentence. Then write the sentence.

looked
helped

The brother _____ the sister.

1. _____

woman
family

The _____ yelled.

2. _____

looked
helped

The sister _____ at the apple.

3. _____

man
car

The _____ walked to work.

4. _____

Instructor's Notes: Review the ten sight words from pages 40-43. For C, read the sight words and the directions together.

Sight Words

bed ● get ● nurse
well ● sick

A. Read the new words above with your teacher.

B. Look at the picture. Read each word.

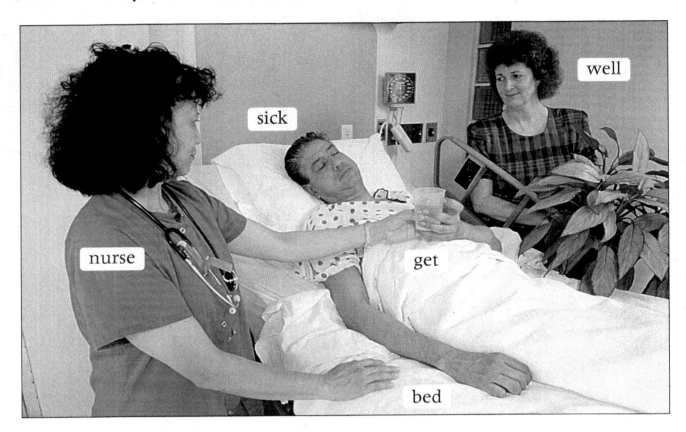

C. Listen to your teacher read the story. Try to read it as you listen. Then circle the new words from the picture. Read each word.

The man in bed is sick.

The nurse takes care of him.

A friend brings a plant to wish him well.

He will get well soon.

Then he can go home.

Instructor's Notes: Introduce new words. Discuss the picture and have students predict what the story is about; discuss predictions later. Read the story aloud and ask students to circle the new words. Have them think of a word that means the opposite of *sick (well)*.

A. Read the words on page 48. Use the picture to help you.

B. Listen to your teacher say each word. Write the new word that rhymes with it.

1. pick ___sick___   **2.** purse _____   **3.** tell _____

4. red _____   **5.** bet _____

C. Write the new word that goes with each picture.

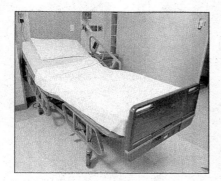

1. _____

4. _____

2. _____

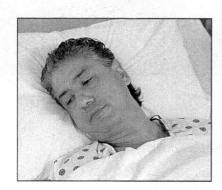

3. _____

5. _____

D. Write a sentence using one of the new words. Your teacher will help you.

_____

_____

Instructor's Notes: Read the five new words and have student repeat them. Then read the directions together. For B, read the five words aloud. For D, help as needed.

49

Unit 3

Sight Words

bus ● city ● like
pay ● store

A. Read the new words above with your teacher.

B. Look at the picture. Read each word.

city

bus

store

like

pay

**C. Listen to your teacher read the story. Try to read it as you listen.
Then circle the new words from the picture. Read each word.**

Here is a busy street in the city.

A man runs from the store.

He wants to ride the bus.

A woman will pay for a paper.

Then she will get on the bus.

Instructor's Notes: Introduce new words. Discuss the picture and have students predict what
the story is about; discuss predictions later. Read the story aloud and ask students to circle the
new words. Have them think of words that mean the opposite of *city (country)* and *like (dislike)*.

50

Unit 3

A. Read the words on page 50. Use the picture to help you.

B. Listen to your teacher say each word. Write the new word that rhymes with it.

1. bike _____

2. say _____

3. more _____

4. us _____

5. pity _____

C. Write the new word that goes with each picture.

1. _____

2. _____

3. _____

4. _____

5. _____

D. Write a sentence using one of the new words. Your teacher will help you.

_____

_____

Instructor's Notes: Read the five new words and have students repeat them. Then read the directions together. For B, read the five words aloud. For D, help as needed.

51

Unit 3

bills ● boss ● job
light ● people

A. Read the new words above with your teacher.

B. Look at the picture. Read each word.

C. Listen to your teacher read the story. Try to read it as you listen. Then circle the new words from the picture. Read each word.

These people need help from the boss.

They are learning a new job.

The boss is telling them how to pay the bills.

They are looking at the bills to pay this month.

The light helps them see well.

Instructor's Notes: Introduce new words. Discuss the picture and have students predict what the story is about; discuss predictions later. Read the story aloud and ask students to circle the new words. Have them think of a word that means the opposite of *light (dark)*.

A. Read the words on page 52. Use the picture to help you.

B. Write the missing letter in each new word. Then write the word.

1. b____lls

   _____

2. b____ss

   _____

3. p____ople

   _____

4. j____b

   _____

5. l____ght

   _____

C. Listen to your teacher say each sentence. Then write the missing word.

1. Turn off the _____ when you go home.

2. My _____ helps me at work.

3. We pay our _____ on time.

4. Are you looking for a new _____ ?

5. Six _____ came in to ask about this job.

D. Write a sentence with each of the new words. Your teacher will help you.

1. _____

2. _____

3. _____

4. _____

5. _____

Instructor's Notes: For A, read the five new words and have students repeat them. Then read the directions for B together. For C, read each sentence to students. For D, help as needed.

53

Unit 3

 ## Adding **-ing** to Action Words

A. Add -ing to each word. Then write the new word.

1. walk + **ing** = walk_____   _____

2. pay + **ing** = pay_____   _____

3. look + **ing** = look_____   _____

4. help + **ing** = help_____   _____

5. yell + **ing** = yell_____   _____

6. work + **ing** = work_____   _____

7. go + **ing** = go_____   _____

8. do + **ing** = do_____   _____

B. Read these words. Then underline the words that go with the picture.

1. a woman looking

2. the people yelling

3. the man paying

4. the dog walking

5. a sister working

6. the boss going

Instructor's Notes: To introduce the concept of adding *-ing* to present tense verbs, write and read to students: *I walk. I am walking. I walked.* Ask which describes the action you are doing right now. For A and B, read the directions together and help students complete the activities.

54

Unit 3

C. Look at each picture. Then read the sentences. Write the word that goes with each picture.

1.

going
working

The sister is

_____ to school.

2.

helping
paying

He is _____

for the food.

3.

walking
looking

She is _____

at the man.

D. Write the word that goes with each picture in the space beneath it.

walking   paying   looking   helping   yelling   working

1.

_____

2.

_____

3.

_____

4.

_____

5.

_____

6.

_____

Instructor's Notes: For C, read the sight words and the directions together. For D, read the directions and the picture names with students.

Review   Pages 48-55

A. Look at each picture. Then read the sentences. Write the word that goes with each picture.

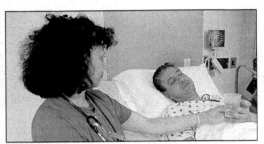

1. People _____ bills.
   pay   like

2. A nurse helps a _____ man.
   sick   store

3. The man _____ a job.
   go   gets

4. The city _____ runs well.
   bus   bed

B. Look at each picture. Then read the words. Underline the words that go with the picture. Then write the words.

a man buying food
a man buying a car

the boss working
the boss paying

a woman walking
a bed walking

1. _____   **2.** _____   **3.** _____

Instructor's Notes: Review the fifteen sight words from pages 48–53. Have students make up a sentence for each word. For A and B, read the directions to students and discuss the pictures.

56

Unit 3

C. **Read the story. Then choose a word to complete each sentence. Write the word.**

bed   job   store   bus   city   boss   people   well   likes

1. Ed got out of _____ early.

2. He had a new _____ .

3. He was going to work at a _____ .

4. Ed got on the _____ .

5. He rode into the _____ .

6. Ed's new _____ showed him what to do.

7. Ed helps _____ find things.

8. Ed's boss says he does _____ .

9. Ed _____ his new job.

D. **Add -ing to each word. Then write the new word.**

1. work + **ing** = work_____   _____

2. help + **ing** = help_____   _____

3. go   + **ing** = go_____   _____

4. yell + **ing** = yell_____   _____

5. look + **ing** = look_____   _____

6. pay   + **ing** = pay_____   _____

7. walk + **ing** = walk_____   _____

Instructor's Notes: Review the fifteen sight words from pages 48–53. For C, read the sentences together and help students choose words to complete them. For D, read the directions and discuss the first item together.

Unit 3 Review

A. Read the words in the word box. Then write the missing letter for each new word.

car	bills	city	job	light	nurse
like	people	stop	well	walk	home

1. st____p

2. cit____

3. lik____

4. w____ll

5. ____ar

6. pe____ple

7. b____lls

8. w____lk

9. ____ob

10. ____ight

11. h____me

12. ____urse

B. Read the words in the word boxes. Then read the sentences. Write the word that best completes each sentence.

1. The man and _____ pay bills.

2. A nurse helps _____ people.

3. Sick people go to _____ .

4. The _____ walks home.

5. The sister _____ at the brother.

6. The man pays for the _____ .

woman	dog

use	sick

radio	bed

van	man

yells	buys

van	money

Instructor's Notes: Read the sight words and directions together. Have students work independently.

C. Add -s or -es to each word. Then write the new word.

1. pay____ _____   2. work____ _____

3. do____ _____   4. watch____ _____

5. stop____ _____   6. run____ _____

7. fix____ _____   8. sit____ _____

9. walk____ _____   10. go____ _____

D. Add -ed to each word. Then write the new word.

1. help____ _____   2. yell____ _____

3. look____ _____   4. walk____ _____

5. work____ _____   6. fix____ _____

E. Add -ing to each word. Then write the new word.

1. look_____ _____

2. work_____ _____

3. go_____ _____

4. pay_____ _____

5. help_____ _____

6. walk_____ _____

7. do_____ _____

8. yell_____ _____

Instructor's Notes: For C, D, and E, read the directions together. Have students work independently. Then assign *Reading for Today Workbook One*, Unit 3.

a ● an ● the

A. Read the new words. Use the pictures to help you.

1. a man
the man

2. a car
the car

3. a bus
the bus

4. a woman
the woman

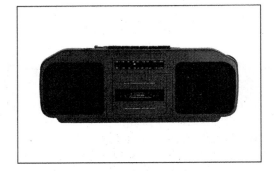

5. a radio
the radio

6. a key
the key

B. Read the word. Then say the name of the picture.

1. an

2. an

3. an

Instructor's Notes: Introduce the new words and have students read after you. Identify the picture names. For A, read the phrases with students. Have students think of sentences using the phrases. For B, explain that we use the word *an* before naming words that begin with vowels: *a, e, i, o,* and *u.*

Sight Words   and • he • she

A. Look at each picture. Then read the sentences.

1. **He** runs.
   She runs.
   He and she run.

2. **She** works.
   He works.
   She and he work.

3. **He** stops the car.
   She stops the car.
   He and she stop the car.

4. **She** sits.
   He sits.
   She and he sit.

B. Read these sentences. Write the new words.

1. She sits. ____She____

   He stands. _____

   She sits, and he stands. _____ _____ _____

2. He likes the car. _____

   She likes the van. _____

   He likes the car, and she likes the van. _____ _____ _____

3. He gets the food. _____

   She gets the water. _____

   He gets the food, and she gets the water. _____ _____ _____

Instructor's Notes: Introduce the new words and have students read after you. For A, read the sentences aloud and have students look at the pictures for each. Have students repeat them. Discuss personal pronouns that take the place of names. For B, read the sentences aloud. Have students repeat and write the new words.

61

Unit 4

Sight Words

is ● are ● was ● were

A. Look at each picture. Then read the sentences.

1. The man **is** sick.
   The man and woman **are** sick.

2. The man **is** walking.
   The dog **was** walking.

3. The woman **is** standing.
   The man **was** standing.

4. The man **was** home.
   The man and woman **were** home.

B. Read these sentences. Write the new words.

1. The man is walking. _____

   The woman was walking. _____

   The man and the dog were walking. _____

2. The man was sick. _____

   The woman is sick. _____

   The nurse and the man are well. _____

3. The brother and sister are yelling. _____

   The man was yelling. _____

   The woman is yelling. _____

Instructor's Notes: Introduce the new words and have students read after you. Explain that *is* and *are* indicate something is happening now, and *was* and *were* indicates something happened in the past. For A and B, read each sentence aloud and have students look at the picture. Ask if the action is happening now or in the past.

Sight Words

I ● you ● they

A. Look at each picture. Then read the sentences.

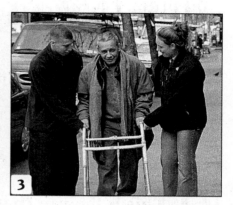

1. **You** and **I** buy food.

2. **I** sit and **you** stand.

3. **They** help the man.

4. **I** look and **they** run.

B. Read these sentences. Write the new words.

1. You and I can get a job. _____ _____

2. I can use the bus. _____

3. They can go home. _____

4. You and I like the car. _____ _____

5. They can pay bills. _____

Instructor's Notes: Introduce the new words and have students read after you. Explain that we use *I* to refer to ourselves, *you* to refer to another person, and *they* to refer to more than one other person. For A, read each sentence aloud and have students look at the picture. Have students repeat the sentences.

63

Unit 4

Sight Words

this ● that ● it

A. Look at each picture. Then read the sentence.

1. **This** is a table, and **that** is an apple.

2. **This** man works, and **that** man helps.

3. **This** is a dog.
   It likes food.

4. **This** is the van **that** I like.
   It runs well.

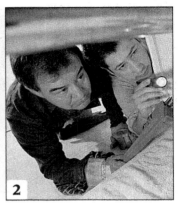

B. Read these sentences. Write the new words.

1. This food bill is big. _____

   I can pay it. _____

2. This man works. _____

   That job pays big money. _____

3. He likes this home, and she likes that home. _____ _____

4. She uses that car, and she likes it. _____ _____

5. Use this money and buy that radio. _____ _____

Instructor's Notes: Introduce the new words and have students read after you. Explain that *this* and *that* are used to point out specific items. *This* is used to point to things closer and *that* is used for things farther away. *It* is used in place of a naming word. For A and B, read the sentences aloud and have students repeat them.

A. Look at each picture. Then read the sentences. Write the word that best completes each sentence.

1. _____ is a man.
   He   She

2. _____ walk.
   They   This

3. The man _____ woman
   a   and

   are standing.

4. She uses _____ key.
   the   I

5. That _____ a car.
   it   is

6. I _____ standing.
   was   you

Instructor's Notes: Review the sixteen sight words from pages 60-64. Read the directions to students. For each item, have students look at the picture and then read each word choice aloud in the sentence to see if it makes sense. Help students read the sentences.

65

Unit 4

B. Look at the words in the word box. Then read the sentences. Write the word that best completes each sentence.

1. The sister ___was___ home.

   _____ was working.

2. _____ is a man.

   _____ is a woman.

   _____ are people.

was	A
She	

She	They
Are	He

3. This is _____ zipper.

   _____ is big.

   _____ use it.

It	a
I	Was

4. _____ you a nurse?

   _____ she sick?

   _____ are well.

You	Is
Are	An

5. That is _____ money.

   I pay you the money, _____ you work.

   _____ work is a job.

That	and
the	I

C. Read this paragraph. Underline the new words from the box.

   We are going. I can use this van. He and she can use the car. You can use the bus. They are walking to the car.

and	the
You	this

Instructor's Notes: Review the sixteen sight words from pages 60–64. For B, read the directions and sentences with students. Discuss the first item. For C, explain that a *paragraph* is a group of sentences that tell about one idea. Point out that a paragraph is indented at the beginning. Read the directions and the paragraph with students.

66

Unit 4

More Practice   you are ● he is ● she is

A. Read the sentences. Write the new words.

1. **You are** working.
   She is working.

   You are buying food.   ___You___ ___are___

   She is buying food.   _____ _____

2. **You are** paying a bill.
   He is paying a bill.
   You and he **are** paying bills.

   You are walking.   _____ _____

   He is walking.   _____ _____

   You and he are walking.   _____ _____ _____

B. Read the sentences. Write the sentences that go with the picture.

1. You are sick.
   He is well.
   They are well.

2. You are going home.
   He is going home.
   You and he are going home.

_____

_____

_____

Instructor's Notes: Introduce the phrases and have students read after you. For A, read the sentences aloud with students. For B, point out that only one group of sentences goes with the photo. Read the sentences aloud.

67

Unit 4

More Practice   they are ● they were ● that is

A. Read the sentences. Write the new words.

1. **They are** yelling.
   That is the woman yelling.

   They are working.   _____ _____

   That is a working man.   _____ _____

2. **They were** paying the bill.
   That is the man paying the bill.
   That is the bill I pay.

   They were helping.   _____ _____

   That is the man helping the dog.   _____ _____

   That is the woman I helped.   _____ _____

B. Read these sentences. Write the sentences that go with the picture.

1. That is the woman I like.
   That is the man I helped.
   They were walking.

2. That is the money.
   That is the light bill.
   They are paying the light bill.

   _____

   _____

   _____

   _____

Instructor's Notes: Introduce the phrases and have students read after you. For A and B, read the directions and the sentences aloud with students.

68

Unit 4

More Practice   she and I ● this is

A. Read the sentences. Write the new words.

1. **This is** the bus.
   She and I use the bus.
   This is the bus **she and I** use.

   This is the boss.   _____ _____

   This is the store.   _____ _____

   She and I work.   _____ _____ _____

2. **This is** a woman.
   She and I walk.
   She and I like walking.

   This is a car.   _____ _____

   This is the car key.   _____ _____

   She and I use the car.   _____ _____ _____

B. Read these sentences. Write the sentences that go with the picture.

1. This is the car that I like.
   She and I use the car.

2. She and I buy the food.
   This is the food the family likes.

_____

_____

_____

_____

Instructor's Notes: Introduce the phrases and have students read after you. Review that *she*
and *I* are personal pronouns that take the place of names. For A and B, read the sentences
aloud with students.

69

Unit 4

More Practice   it was ● a ● the ● they were

A. Read the sentences. Write the new words.

1. **A** man walks.
   The bus stops.

   The city was big.   _____ _____

   It was a big city.   _____ _____ _____

2. **The** people work.
   A boss pays **the** people.

   The brother stands.   _____

   The sister sits.   _____

3. **The** lights were working.
   They were lights that worked well.

   The people walked.   _____

   They were walking.   _____ _____

B. Read these sentences. Write the sentences that go with the picture.

1. The table was big.
   It was the family table.

2. The people were standing.
   The cars were going.

_____

_____

_____

Instructor's Notes: Introduce the phrases and review sight words *a* and *the*. Explain the difference between *a* and *the*: *a* refers to any object and *the* refers to a specific object. Have the student read after you. For A and B, read the sentences aloud with students.

More Practice   this was ● that was

A. Read the sentences. Write the new words.

1. This was the woman, and **that was** the man.

This was the bill, and _____ _____

that was the money. _____ _____

2. That was the sister, and **this was** the brother.

This was the bus, and _____ _____

that was the car. _____ _____

3. That was tea, and **this was** water.

This was the city, and _____ _____

that was the country. _____ _____

B. Read these sentences. Write the sentences that go with the picture.

1. That was a home.
This was a home.

2. This was the man I helped.
That was the woman I helped.

3. That was the bus.
This was the car.

_____

_____

_____

Instructor's Notes: Introduce the phrases and have students read after you. Contrast *this was* and *that was,* which describe the past, to *this is* and *that is,* which describe the present. For A and B, read the sentences aloud with students.

A. Look at each picture. Then read the sentences. Write the word or words that complete each sentence.

1. _____ a car.
   This is   You are

   _____ going.
   The   It was

2. _____ a van.
   That is   You are

   _____ like the van.
   A   She and I

3. This is _____ dog.
   it was   a

   _____ walking the dog.
   That was   He is

4. They buy _____ radio.
   the   that was

   _____ paying the money.
   They are   This was

Instructor's Notes: Read the directions to students. For each item, have students look at the picture and then say each choice aloud in the sentence to see which choice makes better sense. Help students read the sentences.

B. Look at the words in the word box. Then read the sentences. Write the word or words that complete each sentence.

1. _____ walking the dog.

   _____ a big job.

You are
The
This is

2. _____ a nurse.

   _____ helped the nurse.

She and I
He is
A

3. The man was paying _____ bill.

   _____ a big bill.

They are
It was
a

4. _____ a big van.

   _____ buying the van.

   It is _____ van I liked.

They are
the
That is
She and I

5. _____ buying an apple.

   She and I are buying _____ radio.

This was
a
He is

C. Read this paragraph.
Underline the new words from the word box.

We are paying bills. That is the light bill. She and I are paying it. That is the food bill. They are paying that bill. You can help pay the bills.

That is
the
She and I
They are

Instructor's Notes: For B, read the directions and the sentences with students. Have students read the words in the boxes aloud and then choose the one that makes the most sense in each sentence. For C, read the directions and the paragraph with students.

with ● us ● for
has ● who

A. Look at each picture. Read each sentence. Then write the new words.

1. Who sits **with** the woman?

_____ _____

2. The bus stops **for** the light.

_____

3. The woman **has** water.

_____

4. Who runs **with us**?

_____ _____ _____

B. Read these sentences. Underline the new words.

1. The brother walks with us.
He has a sister.
The sister walks with us.
She has a radio.

2. The man sits with us.
He has a dog.
The woman sits with us.
She walks with us.

3. The dog has a home.
He sits for us.
He runs with us.
He likes us.

4. Who works with us?
Who works for money?
The boss has money.
The boss pays us for working.

Instructor's Notes: Introduce the new words and have students read after you. Introduce the use of the question mark as end punctuation for questions. For A, read the sentences and look at the pictures with students. For B, read the sentences with students.

Sight Words

to ● him ● her
them ● why ● does

A. Look at each picture. Read each sentence. Then write the new words.

1. Why does the dog sit with **him**?

_____ _____ _____

2. Why does the van stop for **them**?

_____ _____ _____

3. Why is he standing with **her**?

_____ _____

4. Why does the man walk **to** work?

_____ _____ _____

B. Read the sentences. Underline the new words.

1. The man helps her.
The woman helps him.

2. He walks to work with her.
She walks to work with him.
They go to work with them.

3. This woman walks to work.
She likes her job.
The boss pays her well.
Why does she like her boss?
She likes working for her.

4. She buys food for them.
Does she buy it for him?

Instructor's Notes: Introduce the new words and have students read after you. Review the use of the question mark. For A, read the sentences and look at the pictures with students. Have students suggest possible answers to the questions. For B, read the sentences with students.

Sight Words

by ● from ● me
we ● when

A. Look at each picture. Read each sentence. Then write the new words.

1. Stop the car for **me**.

_____

2. You can sit **by me**.

_____ _____

3. I get the key **from** the table.

_____

4. **When** can **we** go to the store?

_____ _____

B. Read these sentences. Underline the new words.

1. Get the money from me.
   When can you go for me?
   The money is by the bed.
   You can go to the store for me.

2. He works with me.
   He and I get money by working.
   We get the money from the boss.
   When can we get the money?

3. He can go home from work.
   He can walk with me to the
      bus stop.
   We stand by the bus stop.

4. We walk by the store.
   We get food from the store.
   The food is for you and me.
   We like the food store.

Instructor's Notes: Introduce the new words and have student read after you. Point out that
by and *buy* sound the same but have different spellings and different meanings. (*by*: "next to,"
"go past"; *buy*: "to purchase") For A and B, read the sentences with students.

Sight Words   am • not • at
have • cannot

A. Look at each picture. Read the sentences. Then write the new words.

1. I **am** looking **at** the dog.
   He is **not** looking **at** the dog.

_____ _____

2. I **am** working.
   You are **not** working.

_____ _____

3. I **cannot** buy the food.
   I **cannot** make it work.

_____ _____

4. I **have** a car.
   The car is **at** home.

_____ _____

B. Read these sentences. Underline the new words.

1. I have a home.
   I am going home.
   I am not at work.

2. I have bills to pay.
   I have money to pay them.
   I am paying the bills.

3. I am going to work.
   I cannot walk to work.
   I am standing at the bus stop.

4. I am at the store.
   I cannot buy a radio.
   I have bills to pay.

Instructor's Notes: Introduce the new words and have students read after you. Point out that *cannot* is made of two smaller words. For A, read the sentences and look at the pictures with students. For B, read the sentences with students.

Sight Words

both ● in ● no
of ● where

A. Look at each picture. Read each sentence. Then write the new words.

1. The man has **no** key.
   Where is it?

_____ _____

2. **Where** is the key?
   It is **in** the van.

_____

3. **Both of** the sisters are walking.

_____ _____

4. **Both of** them use quarters.

_____ _____

B. Read these sentences. Underline the new words.

1. We are in the store.
   Both of us have money.
   He has no money.

2. Both of us like the country.
   We have no work in the country.
   Both of us work in the city.

3. Both of us have cars.
   Where can we go?
   Both of us go to the city.

4. Both of us have quarters.
   Both of us use the quarters.
   Where is the food?

Instructor's Notes: Introduce the new words and have students read after you. For A, read the sentences and look at the pictures with students. Review the use of the question mark. For B, read the sentences with students.

A. Look at each picture. Then read the sentences.
Write the word that best completes each sentence.

1. Both _____ them like to walk.
   of   to

   _____ people go for a walk
   Both   By

   with the dog.

2. The brothers work _____
   at   from

   the store.

   They work _____ us.
   them   with

3. We have _____ money
   no   am

   to pay the food bill.

   He _____ money to
   him   has

   buy us food.

4. He _____ get the car
   cannot   cat

   to go.

   _____ he work by us?
   Dogs   Does

Instructor's Notes: Read the directions to students. For each item, have students look at
the picture and then say each choice aloud in the sentence to see which choice makes better
sense. Help students read the sentences.

B. Look at the words in the word box. Then read the sentences. Write the word that completes each sentence.

1. I _____ working with people at a country store.

   A woman working with _____ has a family.

   _____

   | us |
   | am |

2. Her family _____ a big home.

   She walked _____ it with me.

   _____

   | has |
   | by |

3. She likes _____ job at the store.

   She likes to work _____ people.

   _____

   | with |
   | her |

4. The store is _____ the country.

   _____ like to walk to work.

   Her dog walks with _____ to the store.

   | We |
   | in |
   | us |

C. Read these paragraphs. Underline the words in each paragraph that are in the word boxes.

Her family helps at home. The brother gets money for helping with the work. He gets money from the sisters. Both of them pay him to work.

| to | at |
| him | them |

The sisters have jobs at the food store. They are not at home. Both of them have cars to get to work.

| Both | them |
| not | have | of |

The brother has no car. He uses the bus. He pays for the bus with the money he gets from his sisters.

| for | no |
| from | with |

Instructor's Notes: For B, read the directions and the sentences with students. For C, read the directions and the story with students. Ask students to summarize the story.

80

Unit 4

More Practice   at ● am ● from ● him

A. Read the sentences. Write the new words.

1. I **am** standing **at** the bus stop.   _____ _____

   I **am** going to work.   _____

   I **am** sick of going to work.   _____

2. I **am** working for a boss.   _____

   I get money **from him** for working.   _____ _____

   I go home **from** work with **him**.   _____ _____

3. I **am** going to the food store with **him**.   _____ _____

   I **am** going **from** work.   _____ _____

   I **am** going to buy food **at** the store   _____ _____

   with **him**.   _____

B. Read these sentences. Write the sentences that go with the picture.

1. The woman is looking at the car.
   The man is looking at the car.

2. She is looking at him.
   He is looking at her.

3. She is walking with him.
   I am walking with them.

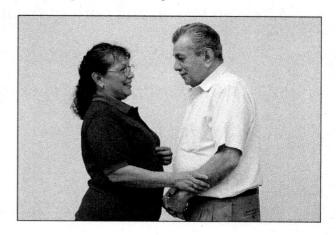

_____

_____

Instructor's Notes: Read the sight words aloud and have students read after you. For A and B, read the directions and the sentences aloud with students. Explain that the phrase *sick of going to work* means "tired of going to work."

81

Unit 4

More Practice both ● by ● of ● them

A. Read the sentences. Write the new words.

1. They are going **by** car.   _____

2. **Both of them** use the car
   to go to the store.   _____ _____ _____

3. **Both of** us are going with   _____ _____

   them.   _____

4. **Both** sisters have dogs.   _____

5. **Both of them** walk the   _____ _____ _____

   dogs **by** the water.   _____

B. Read these sentences. Write the sentence that goes with the picture.

1. People get bills, and people pay them.

2. Both people are sick, and the nurse helps them.

3. We go by car, and both of them go by bus.

4. Both dogs like walking by the water.

5. They work with both of the sisters.

6. Both of the homes are new.

_____

_____

_____

Instructor's Notes: Read the sight words aloud and have students read after you. For A and B, read the directions and the sentences aloud with students. Ask students to think of more sentences using the words.

More Practice   we • us • not • with • cannot

A. Read the sentences. Write the new words.

1. **We** are sick in bed and   _____

   cannot go to work.   _____

   We are **not** well; **we** are   _____ _____ _____
   at home.

2. Are you working **with us**?   _____ _____

   He is **not** working **with**   _____ _____

   us; he is helping the boss.   _____

3. **We** can walk **with** him to   _____ _____
   the bus stop.

   She **cannot** walk **with us**;   _____ _____ _____
   she is going by car.

B. Read these sentences. Write the sentences that go with the picture.

1. We are going to the bus stop.
   Can we use this bus to get to work?

2. She is not going with us.
   She is going to work in her car.

3. They cannot go to work with us.
   They are walking with him.

_____

_____

Instructor's Notes: Read the sight words aloud and have students read after you. For A and B, read the directions and the sentences aloud with students. Explain the semicolons used in the sentences in A: a punctuation mark that is used where you could use a period, but you want to show that the two sentences are closely related.

More Practice   have ● no ● has ● in

A. Read the sentences. Write the new words.

1. I **have no** car keys with me.   _____ _____

   She **has** the keys **in** her home.   _____ _____

   I cannot get **in** the car.   _____

   She **has** to go home and get the keys.   _____

2. **No**, I cannot get **in** the water with you.   _____ _____

   I **have** to go home and go to work.   _____

   She **has** to go with me and help me   _____
   with the job.

B. Read the sentences. Write the sentences that go with the picture.

1. The dog has her food.
   I have water for her.

2. She works in a store.
   He has no work.

3. The family has a home.
   The brother works in the home.

_____

_____

_____

Instructor's Notes: Read the sight words aloud and have students read after you. For A and B, read the directions and the sentences aloud with students.

More Practice   for ● her ● me ● to

A. Read the sentences. Write the new words.

1. I am looking **for her**; I have money **for her**.

_____ _____

_____ _____

She can use the money from **me to** pay **her** bills.

_____ _____ _____

2. This zipper is **for me to** use.

_____ _____ _____

The quarters are **for her to** buy dog food.

_____ _____ _____

3. Go **to** the store **for me** and get the food.

_____ _____ _____

I like **her**, and I am buying a radio **for her**.

_____ _____ _____

B. Read the sentences. Write the sentences that go with the picture.

1. The boss pays me to work.
I pay her to help me.

2. She uses her money to buy food.
The food is for her family.

3. I use the money to pay the light bill.
I use the desk to work at home.

_____

_____

_____

Instructor's Notes: Read the sight words aloud and have students read after you. For A and B, read the directions and the sentences aloud with students.

A. Look at each picture. Then read the sentences. Write the word that best completes each sentence.

1. _____ of us go for a walk.
   Both   Them

   She _____ go with us.
      her   cannot

   _____ walk the dog for her.
   We   From

2. They stand _____ the van.
                    by   am

   I _____ not going with them.
      of   am

   I am going _____ work.
                    to   me

3. I _____ her keys.
     have   him

   She is not _____ home.
                 at   us

   _____ dog is at home.
   In   Her

4. She _____ a big job to do.
          has   in

   _____ sister helps.
   She   Her

   They _____ work.
            both   us

Instructor's Notes: Read the directions with students. For each item, have students look at the picture and then say each word choice aloud in the sentence to see which makes better sense. Help students read the sentences. Ask students to make up a story about one of the pictures.

B. Look at the words in the word box. Read the sentences. Write the word that best completes each sentence.

1. _____ are going from work to the store.

   That man is going with _____ .

   He is _____ going home.

<table>
<tr><td>We</td></tr>
<tr><td>not</td></tr>
<tr><td>us</td></tr>
</table>

2. In the store they _____ zippers.

   I looked _____ this zipper.

   I _____ buying it for her.

<table>
<tr><td>am</td></tr>
<tr><td>have</td></tr>
<tr><td>at</td></tr>
</table>

3. We can walk home _____ the store.

   You can go home with _____ .

   The man can go home _____ bus.

<table>
<tr><td>me</td></tr>
<tr><td>from</td></tr>
<tr><td>by</td></tr>
</table>

C. Read these paragraphs. Underline the words in each paragraph that are in the word boxes.

This man and I work in the city. Both of us walk home from work.

We stop by the home of a sick family. The man has food for them. He pays the bills for them.

The family likes him. He is like a brother to the people in this family. He has no family in this city.

<table>
<tr><td>Both</td><td>from</td></tr>
<tr><td>of</td><td>us</td></tr>
</table>

<table>
<tr><td>them</td><td>for</td></tr>
<tr><td>by</td><td>has</td></tr>
</table>

<table>
<tr><td>him</td><td>in</td></tr>
<tr><td>no</td><td>this</td></tr>
</table>

Instructor's Notes: For B, read the directions and the sentences with students. Have students read the words in the boxes aloud and then choose the one that fits in each sentence. For C, read the directions and the story with students. Have students summarize the story.

87

Unit 4

Sight Words

your • so • very

A. Look at each picture. Read each sentence. Then write the new word or words.

1. He works **so** hard.

_____

2. The woman runs **very** fast.

_____

3. Is this **your** dog?

_____

4. Is **your** brother **very** tall?

_____   _____

B. Read these sentences. Underline the new words.

1. The light is so bright.
The light is very bright.

2. Is your street very long?
My street is so long I can't see
the end.
It is a very quiet street.

3. I love my dog so much.
Is your dog very small?
I like very small dogs.

4. Is she your teacher?
The teacher is very nice.
I am so glad she is my teacher.

Instructor's Notes: Introduce the new words and have students read after you. For A, read the
sentences and look at the pictures with students. For B, read the sentences with students.

88   Unit 4

Sight Words

been • would • ask • if

A. Look at each picture. Read each sentence. Then write the new word or words.

1. **Would** you **ask** her to sit down?

_____ _____

2. **Ask** him **if** he has **been** to the store.

_____ _____ _____

3. She has **been** in the water.

_____

4. He **asked if** she **would** help.

_____ _____ _____

B. Read these sentences. Underline the new words.

1. Where has she been?
   I wonder if she has been home.
   Would you ask her?

2. He has been sick.
   He will get well if he stays
   in bed.

3. I have not been to the park.
   Would she like to go to the park?
   I would like for her to come.
   I will ask her.

4. She has been at work.
   She will have fun if she comes.

Instructor's Notes: Introduce the new words and have students read after you. For A, read the sentences and look at the pictures with students. For B, read the sentences with students.

Sight Words

up ● yes ● their

A. Look at each picture. Read each sentence. Then write the new word or words.

1. He is going **up their** stairs.

_____ _____

2. **Yes**, I will come to the party.

_____

3. **Yes, their** home is nice.

_____ _____

4. I can get **up** on the rock.

_____

B. Read these sentences. Underline the new words.

1. Their house is up the hill.
   Yes, it is very high.
   They must climb up the hill
   every day.

2. They asked her to their party.
   She said yes.

3. The stairs go up to the sixth
   floor.
   Their office is on the third floor.

4. Their plane will land soon.
   Can you see it up in the sky?
   Yes, I can see it.

Unit 4

Review Pages 88-90

A. Look at each picture. Then read the sentences. Write the word that best completes each sentence.

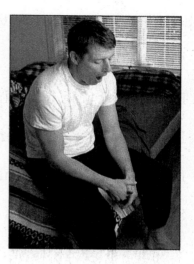

1. Is this _____ house?
your   year

_____ , it is my house.
No   Yes

2. He has _____ sleeping.
bed   been

He slept _____ late.
very   vase

3. They asked _____ she
if   it

wanted to sit down.

She said she _____ like
would   was

to sit.

4. He climbed _____ high.
as   so

How far _____ did he climb?
in   up

Instructor's Notes: Review the ten sight words from pages 88-90. For A, read the directions with students. For each item, have students look at the picture and then say each choice aloud in the sentence to see which choice makes better sense. Help students read the sentences.

91

Unit 4

More Practice   your ● so ● very

A. Read the sentences. Write the new words.

1. **Your** cat is **so** pretty.   _____ _____

   Does **your** dog like him?   _____

   He likes to sit on **your** steps.   _____

   He is a **very** happy cat.   _____

2. She is **so** glad she has a day off.   _____

   She works **very** hard.   _____

   She brings **your** mail every day.   _____

3. **Your** work was **very** good.   _____ _____

   Will **your** boss like it?   _____

   Your family will be **so** proud.   _____ _____

B. Read these sentences. Write the sentences that go with the picture.

1. He is very sad.
   She is also sad.

2. He is walking away from her.
   She is looking at him.

3. He is very happy.
   She is very happy, too.

_____

_____

Instructor's Notes: Review the sight words and have students read after you. For A and B, read the sentences aloud with students.

More Practice   been ● would ● ask ● if

A. Read the sentences. Write the new words.

1. He **asked if** she had **been** to the store. _____ _____ _____

    She had **been** to school. _____

    She **would** go to the store **if** he **asked**. _____ _____ _____

2. He **would** do well **if** he worked. _____ _____

    He has **been** working hard. _____

    He **asked** his brother to help him. _____

3. **Would** you come with us? _____

    Did she **ask** you to come next time? _____

    I will come with you, **if** you like. _____

B. Read these sentences. Write the sentences that go with the picture.

1. The woman has not been to the store. The man has been to the store.

2. They are asking the man to come. I am asking the man to come.

3. The woman has been to the store. The man has not been to the store.

_____

_____

_____

Instructor's Notes: Review the sight words and have students read after you. For A, read the sentences aloud with students. For B, point out that only one group of sentences goes with the photo. Read the sentences aloud.

More Practice   up ● yes ● their

A. Read the sentences. Write the new words.

1. **Their** baseball is **up** on the roof.   _____ _____

   Yes, he will go **up** and get it.   _____ _____

   He throws **their** ball down.   _____

2. She asked him to help her **up**.   _____

   He said **yes**.   _____

   Their work was good.   _____

3. How high **up** is the plane?   _____

   The plane went **up** in the air.   _____

   Their plane is coming.   _____

B. Read these sentences. Write the sentences that go with the picture.

1. Their dog is walking.
   It is walking up the street.

2. Their cat is up in a tree.
   Yes, I will go get it.

3. He is up on the hill.
   Yes, it is very high.

_____

_____

_____

Instructor's Notes: Review the sight words and have students read after you. For A, read the sentences aloud with students. For B, point out that only one group of sentences goes with the photo. Read the sentences aloud.

94

Unit 4

A. Look at each picture. Then read the sentences. Write the word that best completes each sentence.

1. _____ you cut the cake?
   Would   Very

   She says _____ .
   yes   yet

2. He has _____ looking for her.
   big   been

   She _____ if she can help.
   and   asks

3. Are these _____ bicycles?
   yard   your

   These are _____ bicycles.
   that   their

4. _____ you go too high,
   If   In

   you might fall.

Instructor's Notes: Read the directions to students. For each item, have the student look at the picture and then say each choice aloud in the sentence to see which choice makes better sense. Help students read the sentences.

Number Words   zero   one   two   three   four   five

A. Look at the pictures. Read the words and numbers.
Write the number word by the picture.

zero = 0

___zero___

one = 1

_____ home

two = 2

_____ dogs

three = 3

_____ cups

four = 4

_____ people

five = 5

_____ lights

B. Draw a line from the number
to the word.

0 ----------- five
1 ----------- zero
2   four
3   one
4   two
5   three

C. Write the number words in order.

five	two	four
three	zero	one

___zero_____

_____

_____

Instructor's Notes: Introduce the number words and have students read after you. Read each
set of directions to students. Help students complete the exercises. Have students make up
sentences using the words.

six   seven   eight   nine   ten

A. Look at the pictures. Read the words and numbers. Write the number word by the picture.

six = 6

_____ forks

seven = 7

_____ keys

eight = 8

_____ shirts

nine = 9

_____ ants

ten = 10

_____ cars

B. Draw a line from the number to the word.

6	eight
7	nine
8	seven
9	ten
10	six

C. Write the number words in order.

eight   ten   nine
six   seven

_____

_____

_____

Instructor's Notes: Introduce the number words and have students read after you. Read each set of directions to students. Help students complete the exercises. Have students make flash cards of the number words.

A. Write the number that goes with the word.

eight __8__   seven _____   one _____   nine _____

five _____   six _____   two _____   zero _____

four _____   three _____   ten _____

B. Write the word that goes with the number.

3 __three__   6 _____   0 _____

5 _____   2 _____   7 _____

1 _____   4 _____   8 _____

9 _____   10 _____

C. Count the dots. Write the number and the number word under each domino.

   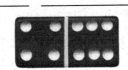   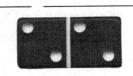

__5__ __five__   _____ _____   _____ _____

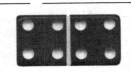   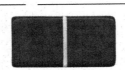   

_____ _____   _____ _____   _____ _____

_____ _____   _____ _____   _____ _____

_____ _____   _____ _____   _____ _____

Instructor's Notes: Read each set of directions to students. For A and B, have students work independently. For C, explain that students must count the total number of dots on each domino.

A. Read the number words in the word box. Write the number words in the correct order.

<u> zero </u>   _____   _____

_____   _____   _____

_____   _____   _____

_____   _____

eight	one
six	nine
ten	four
five	zero
three	two
seven	

B. Read the number words in the word box. Then read the story. Write the number word that completes each sentence.

The Family

The family has two brothers and three sisters.

The family has ____<u>five</u>____ people in it. The family

has _____ home. The home has lights, tables,

beds, and radios. One of the lights is by a table,

and two of them are not. The home has

_____ lights.

one
Ten
three
two
five

Four of the family work at a food store. Six

people work with the family at the store.

_____ people work at the store. Eight of the

people at the store are well, and _____

people are sick.

Instructor's Notes: For A, read the directions with students. For B, explain that students will have to do some simple math to figure out the missing words. Read the story with students.

99

Unit 4

You have learned the number words for counting. There is another kind of number word that tells the order or place something has in a group.

Example: There are <u>two</u> tables. (counting)
            The <u>second</u> table is his. (order)

Read these numbers and their number words.

1	one	first	6	six	sixth
2	two	second	7	seven	seventh
3	three	third	8	eight	eighth
4	four	fourth	9	nine	ninth
5	five	fifth	10	ten	tenth

A. Look at the picture. Write a number word to complete the sentence. Then circle the correct part of the picture.

1. There are ___five___ butterflies.
   Circle the first butterfly.

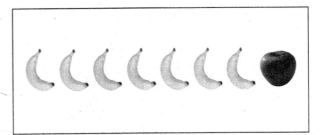

2. There are _____ spoons.
   Circle the sixth spoon.

3. There are _____ boxes.

   Circle the third box.

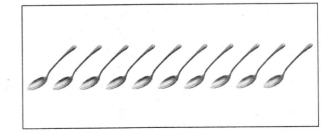

4. There are _____ bananas.

   There is _____ apple.
   Circle the fifth banana.

Instructor's Notes: Read the information in the box with students. Go over each number and its two number words. For A, read the directions and the first item with students. Help students complete the exercise.

B. Look at the pictures and read the sentences. Write a number word to complete each sentence.

1. There are ___three___ cars.

   The ___first___ is red.

2. There are _____ cans.

   The _____ is a can of corn.

3. There are _____ keys.

   The _____ key is big.

4. There are _____ socks.

   The _____ sock is red.

5. There are _____ glasses.

   The _____ glass has milk in it.

6. There are _____ shirts.

   The _____ shirt is blue.

7. There are _____ cups.

   The _____ cup is red.

8. There are _____ dots.

   The _____ dot is yellow.

9. There are _____ clocks.

   The _____ clock is green.

Instructor's Notes: For B, read the directions and the first item with students. Help students complete the exercise.

101

Unit 4

A. The words in each row all begin with the same letter. Write the missing letter.

1. cat   ___an   ___up   ___ap   ___ake   ___one

2. food   ___ork   ___amily   ___rom   ___or   ___ish

3. map   ___oney   ___at   ___ice   ___ule   ___an

4. rug   ___adio   ___obe   ___ake   ___ide   ___ose

B. Write a word that rhymes with each word below.

1. bin   _____

2. bat   _____

3. can   _____

4. fox   _____

C. Below is a list of some of the words you learned in this book. Next to each word, write more words that start with the same letter. You can look through the book to help you.

1. bed   _____

2. can   _____

3. dog   _____

4. food   _____

5. light   _____

6. nurse   _____

7. sister   _____

8. work   _____

Instructor's Notes: Explain that this page reviews many words and sounds. For A, read the directions to students and discuss the first row together. For B and C, read the directions to students. Then encourage them to work independently. Help as needed.

D. Read the words in the word boxes. Then read the sentences.
Write the word that best completes each sentence.

1. She is _____ her dog.

   It is a _____ big dog.

   She _____ before she crosses the street.

   _____

walking
very
stops
so

2. _____ you come to the party?

   _____ will buy a cake.

   Everyone will bring _____ .

   _____

been
She and I
Would
food

3. They are going to the _____ .

   The whole _____ will come.

   You _____ come, too.

   _____

can
sit
county
family

4. They listen to _____ radio.

   The radio is on the _____ .

   _____ my radio.

   _____

they
This is
table
their

5. A _____ takes care of sick people.

   If you are sick, you should stay in _____ .

   Then you will get _____ .

   _____

bed
nurse
this is
well

6. Are you going to the _____ ?

   Take some _____ with you.

   Don't forget your car _____ .

store
keys
money
bus

Instructor's Notes: Explain that this page reviews many sight words. Read the directions together and have students work independently as much as they can. Help as needed.

103

E. Add -s, -es, -ed, or -ing to the words in the sentences. Then write the new word.

1. My brother works on two job_____ . _____

2. The woman is stand_____ up. _____

3. That store sells radio_____ . _____

4. She walk_____ five miles this morning. _____

5. Give me the key_____ . _____

6. Are you go_____ to the party? _____

7. I help_____ make dinner. _____

8. The girl watch_____ TV every day. _____

9. He is look_____ for a new car. _____

10. He work_____ yesterday. _____

11. She yell_____ louder than he does. _____

12. We like help_____ people. _____

F. Read the number words. Look at the picture and read the sentences. Write a number word in each sentence.

one	two	four	five	eight	ten
first	second	fourth	fifth	eighth	tenth

1. The _____ button is red.

2. The _____ button is orange.

3. The _____ button is yellow.

4. The _____ button is blue.

5. There are _____ buttons.

Instructor's Notes: Explain that this page reviews many words and sounds. Read the directions together and have students work independently. For E, students may look back through the book to find similar sentences.

Look at the picture. Read the story. Write the answers to the questions.

Help with a Job

Pam works in the city. She uses a city bus to get to her job. She works at a food store. She likes her job. She likes going to work.

Her brother Ben does not have a job. He cannot go look for one. He has been sick at home for a week. So, Pam stops by to help him. She gets him food. She walks the dog for him. She helps him get well.

Instructor's Notes: Ask students to read the story title, look at the photos, and predict what the story is about. Read each paragraph to students and then have them repeat. Continue reading on page 106.

105

Read a Story

Today Ben gets up and he is not sick. He can walk the dog. He walks to the store to buy food. He walks home with the food.

A car goes by. The woman in the car stops at a light. She works at the food store. She yells to Ben. She asks him if he would like a job. He likes the job and the money. He will go to work today.

Comprehension

Think About It

1. Who was sick?
2. Where does Pam ride a bus?
3. Why does Pam stop by her brother's home?
4. When will Ben go to work?

Instructor's Notes: Ask students to summarize the events. Review the question words *who*, *where*, *when*, and *why*. Then help students read and answer the questions. Then assign *Reading for Today Workbook One*, Unit 4. Use Blackline Master 8: Certificate of Completion from the *Instructor's Guide* to recognize students who successfully complete this book.

Learner Checklist Reading for Today — Book One

Skill	Completion	Skill	Completion	Skill	Completion

Unit 1

b, c, d, f ....☐
g, h, j, k ....☐
l, m, n, p ....☐
qu, r, s, t ....☐
v, w, x, y, z ....☐

Unit 2

Short a ....☐
Long a ....☐
Long a and Short a ....☐
Short i ....☐
Long i ....☐
Long i and Short i ....☐
Read a Story........................☐
Short o.................................☐
Long o ....☐
Long o and Short o............☐
Short u ....☐
Long u ....☐
Long u and Short u ....☐
Read a Story.......................☐
Short e.................................☐
Long e..................................☐
Long e and Short e ....☐
Read a Story......................☐

Unit 3

big, man, run, sit,
    stand ....☐
can, go, stop, food,
    table....................................☐
Writing Skills: Adding –s
    and –es to Action
    Words ....☐
Review ....☐
home, use, key, walk,
    woman ....☐
buy, dog, money,
    radio, yell ....☐
Writing Skills: Adding –s
    and –es to Naming
    Words ....☐
Review ....☐
brother, car, country,
    sister, work ....☐
family, van, look,
    help, water ....☐
Writing Skills: Adding –ed
    to Action Words ....☐
Review ....☐
bed, get, nurse,
    well, sick ....☐
bus, city, like, pay,
    store ....☐
bills, boss, job, light,
    people................................☐
Writing Skills: Adding –ing
    to Action Words ....☐
Review ....☐
Unit 3 Review ....☐

Unit 4

a, an, the ....☐
and, he, she..........................☐
is, are, was, were ....☐
I, you, they.........................☐
this, that, it ....☐
Review ....☐
More Practice....................☐
Review ....☐
with, us, for, has, who ....☐
to, him, her, them,
    why, does ....☐
by, from, me, we,
    when................................☐
am, not, at, have,
    cannot..............................☐
both, in, no, of, where.........☐
Review ....☐
More Practice....................☐
Review ....☐
your, so, very.......................☐
been, would, ask, if.............☐
up, yes, their ....☐
Review ....☐
More Practice....................☐
Review ....☐
Number Words..................☐
Review ....☐
Writing Skills:
    Writing Numbers..........☐
Final Review ....☐
Read a Story.......................☐

Word List

Below is a list of the 272 words (including common endings) in *Book One* of *Reading for Today*. Words with an asterisk following are review words from the lower level *Introductory Book*.

A
a
am
an
and
apple*
are
ask
at*
ax*

B
bat*
bed*
beds
bee*
been
beet*
big*
bike*
bill
bills
boss
both
box*
brother
brothers
bus*
buy
buying
buys
by

C
cage*
cake*
can*
cane*
cannot

cap*
cape*
car*
cars
cat*
city
cone*
cot*
country
cub*
cube*
cup*

D
dam*
desk*
dice*
dime*
dishes*
does
dog*
dogs

E
egg*
eight
eighth

F
family
fan*
fifth
file*
fin*
first
fish*
five*
flag*
food*
for
fork*

four
fourth
fox*
from
fuse*

G
gas*
gate*
get
gets
globe*
go*
going

H
ham*
has
hat*
have
he
help
helped
helping
helps
her
him
hive*
hole*
home*
homes
hug*

I
I
if
in
inch*
is
it

J
jam*
jeans*
jeep*
jet*
job
jobs
June*

K
key*
keys
kite*
kitten*

L
leaf*
lid*
light*
lights
like*
likes
lock*
log*
look
looked
looking
looks

M
man*
map*
mat*
me
meat*
men*
mitt*
money*
mop*
mule*

N
nail*
nest*
net*
nine
ninth
no
nose*
not*
note*
nurse*

O
of
olive*
one
ox*

P
pan*
pay
paying
pays
people*
pill*
pin*
pine*
plum*
pot*

Qu
quarter*
quarters
queen*
quilt*

R
radio*
radios
rake*
rice*

robe*
rod*
rope*
rug*
run*
runs

S
safe*
sea*
seal*
second
seed*
seven
seventh
she
sick*
sister
sisters
sit
sits
six*
sixth
smoke*
so
socks*
stand
standing
stands
stop*
stops
store
stove*
sun*

T
table*
tables
tap
tape*

tax*
tea*
team*
ten
tenth
that
the
their
them
they
third
this
three
tie*
to
today
tote*
tree*
tub*
tube*
tune*
two

U
umbrella*
up
us
use
uses

V
van*
vane*
vase*
very
vet*
vine*

W
walk
walked

walking
walks
was
water*
we
web*
weed*
well
when*
where*
who*
why*
win*
with
woman*
work
worked
working
works
would

Y
yard
yell*
yelled
yelling
yellow
yells
yes
you
your

Z
zero*
zipper*
zippers
zoo*